PROSPERITY WITHOUT GREED

T0351263

About the Author (http://www.sahra-wagenknecht.de/)

Sahra Wagenknecht holds a Ph.D. in economics and is a journalist and politician. Since October 2015 she has been the parliamentary leader of the party Die Linke in the German Bundestag. From 2010 to 2014 she was deputy secretary of her party, from 2004 to 2009 she was a Member of the European Parliament.

About the Translator (http://people.trentu.ca/~apickel/)

Andreas Pickel is a Professor of Global Politics at Trent University in Peterborough, Ontario, Canada. He has published books and articles in the areas of post-communist transformation, nationalism, and the philosophy of the social sciences.

SAHRA WAGENKNECHT

PROSPERITY WITHOUT GREED

How to Save Ourselves from Capitalism

Translated from the German by Andreas Pickel

Campus Verlag
Frankfurt/New York

The original edition was published in 2016 by Campus Verlag under the title
Reichtum ohne Gier. Wie wir uns vor dem Kapitalismus retten. All rights reserved.

ISBN 978-3-593-50758-3 Print
ISBN 978-3-593-43669-2 E-Book (PDF)
ISBN 978-3-593-43670-8 E-Book (EPUB)

Copyright © 2016 Campus Verlag GmbH, Frankfurt-on-Main
Cover design: Guido Klütsch, Cologne
Cover illustration: Paul Schirnhofer Fotografie, Berlin
Typesetting: Campus Verlag GmbH, Frankfurt-on-Main
Fonts: Scala, Scala Sans and Pill Gothic 300mg
Printed in the United States of America

www.campus.de
www.press.uchicago.edu

CONTENTS

PART II
MARKET ECONOMY INSTEAD OF ECONOMIC FEUDALISM:
SKETCH OF A MODERN ECONOMIC ORDER

TRANSLATOR'S FOREWORD

Sahra Wagenknecht is a prominent figure on Germany's political stage. Since 2009 she has been a member of the federal parliament and the party leadership of *Die Linke*. She appears regularly on public affairs talk shows and is frequently in the news. She is one of Germany's intellectually strongest and economically most knowledgeable politicians. While these are not the only, or even main, characteristics of a successful politician, they are all too rare in the country's political class.

Like Chancellor Angela Merkel, Wagenknecht grew up in the former GDR (East Germany). She became politically active just prior to the fall of the Berlin wall in 1989. She is in the leadership of *Die Linke*, currently an opposition party in the German Bundestag with a feminist and socialist orientation. Wagenknecht may well earn a place in the German government, if not after the next elections in the fall of 2017, then at some future time.

Prosperity without Greed is in equal parts political analysis and reform program. It explains in clear and jargon-free terms how today's capitalist economy really works, demonstrating how it runs afoul not only of basic ideas of social justice, but of the principles of a free market economy itself. She shows how today's dominant financial sector functions and how "the one percent" end up with most of society's wealth, for which they do not have to work.

Most importantly, Wagenknecht sketches a vision of an alternative economy, a more genuine market economy without the dominance of private capitalists. While private wealth can still be earned in firms in which the owner remains personally liable, the ownership system of private shareholding, which she characterizes as "neo-feudalism", will be largely replaced by enterprises that are "self-owned"—employee-owned and common-good companies. Wagenknecht's brand of socialism has significant elements of "market radicalism", though clearly not of the neoliberal type which uses market ideology to disguise an anti-market and inegalitarian corporate order.

It is clear by now that successful solutions for climate change-induced problems will need to transcend the capitalist logic of limitless private capital accumulation. The significance of Wagenknecht's work emerges in this context with particular force—a guide for progressive organizations, movements and activists for how the existing economy could be transformed. The book comes at what seems like an inauspicious time for radical reform ideas, with a reactionary U.S. President recently installed in office. But political dynamics tend to be unpredictable, which is why the prospects for radical change of a progressive kind cannot and should not be discounted.

Andreas Pickel, February 2017

PREFACE

The time is out of joint; O curs'd spite,
That ever I was born to set it right!
Hamlet, in Shakespeare's famous tragedy,
surveying the state of his kingdom

Hamlet's attempt to set things right ends in major bloodshed, suggesting that such attempts ought not be imitated. Yet the lesson is not that we should simply accept society's dissolution. Instead, we need to approach the problem in a way that rises to the challenge. Hamlet yearns to return to the good old days. But the future lies in what is new and has never existed before. Ideas for change should be assessed in terms of their plausibility and persuasiveness, not for whether they have a track record of success.

And isn't our own time *out of joint*? Isn't this what the news we hear and read on a daily basis, the online flood of information, tells us? The truth is, we all feel that things cannot and will not continue the way they are. The big question therefore is: what comes next?

Civilization in retreat

In many regions of the world, civilization is in retreat. Wars and civil wars have turned the Middle East and parts of Africa into a blazing firestorm. Public order is collapsing. Clan leaders, war lords, and terror militias are taking control. Fear, chaos, atrocities and arbitrary killings are the result. Pretty much everywhere, the United States and European countries are involved in these conflicts. It's about raw materials and markets, profits and geostrategic advantages, pipeline routes and the competition for power with the West's old opponent, Russia.

More than 60 million people worldwide have lost their homes and have become refugees as a result of such conflicts. Some of them make it to Europe. The majority survive in camps and tent cities located just outside their countries of origin: without work, without a future, without hope, relying on others to feed them and keep them alive.

Even in the advanced industrialized countries—islands of wealth with a comparatively high standard of living—life has become tougher rather than better for many people. Financial bubbles, economic crises, unemployment, dying industrial regions, squalid bedroom communities, jobs that don't pay a living wage, poverty in old age, insecurity—all threaten our daily lives and frighten us.

After us the flood

Who is willing to find new solutions for our time, who has the ability, the courage and the right ideas? And who, conversely, has a secret or not so secret interest in keeping things just the way they are? "Après nous le déluge!"—"after us the flood"—in the words of the legendary mistress of French King Louis XV, Madame de Pompadour, in 1757 when bad news threatened to disrupt one of their lavish court celebrations. For the majority of French people at the time, on the other hand, life was no party—which is why the royal house of Bourbons would experience its own flood thirty years later.

"After us the flood" is not a particularly attractive slogan for those who are up to their necks in water. That was true in the eighteenth century. Is it not true in the same way today? What are we waiting for?

The richest 1 percent of the world population now has more wealth than the other 99 percent. 62 multi-billionaires own more assets than half of humanity combined[1]. At the same time, the inequality of incomes and assets continues to grow, not only on a global scale, but also and especially in the old industrialized countries. Over the past twenty years, the exploding wealth at the top has ceased to pull up the middle class, let alone the poor. Their standard of living does not simply lag behind economic growth, it has become completely disconnected.

The tide that was once supposed to raise all boats now only carries luxury yachts. Since the 1980s, average wages in the United States have stagnated, while lower wages have gone into free fall. In the meantime, Europe has adopted the same model. The upper classes are sitting in their penthouses, elevators on hold and ladders pulled up. The rest are lucky if they manage to continue living on one of the lower floors—which many don't. This is the case not only in crisis-ridden Southern Europe, but also in wealthy Germany with its booming export economy.

Neither hard work and qualifications nor second or third jobs nowadays offer any guarantee of a relatively comfortable existence. Prosperity in the "middle of society", to which political hypocrites like to appeal, has become fragile. Whereas in earlier years individuals were able to rise—if not from dishwasher to millionaire, then at least from a working class background to the middle class—nowadays the typical experience is one of decline. Rarely do children today fare better than their parents, while the opposite is often the case.

The inheritance club

One exception is the exclusive club of heirs who can expect a large inheritance that will insure a good life regardless of their own contributions. The promise of social betterment, a main reason for the popularity of capitalism in the second half of the twentieth century, sounds hollow and has lost credibility. Once again it is social origin rather than talent and personal initiative that determines whether one will reach the upper echelons of society's income and property hierarchy.

Admittedly, jobs with good incomes that afford the classic standard of living of the middle class still do exist. However, for the most part, a high price has to be paid in return: extreme performance pressure, round-the-clock availability, a life devoted to work with little room for family, friends, and leisure. Even for skilled workers and academics, sufficient incomes are no longer standard. A university degree does not protect you from low wages or the permanent insecurity of contract jobs and precarious self-employment. In Southern Europe, young people with top educational credentials face the choice between emigrating or remaining unemployed at home.

The number of people experiencing humiliating poverty in prosperous Europe is increasing. More and more people put only the cheapest products into their shopping carts, spend winters in under-heated apartments, and can only dream of occasionally going to a restaurant or taking a vacation. Perhaps what's even worse is to see your children grow up in run-down apartment complexes such as the banlieues of Paris, where in chronically under-financed schools they learn about violence and crime rather than receiving a good education.

How do we want to live?

Do we really want to keep living this way? Do we want a society in which individuals are becoming increasingly ruthless because everyone is always worried about crashing and joining the army of losers—an army from which all too often there is no return? Do we want that insecurity and fear of the future shape our daily lives while it is sold to us as the new freedom? And if we do not want this, why don't we resist? Why do we tolerate so much—all the imposition, humiliation, and hypocrisy that we see for what they are: simply lies? Why do we accept lives that are so much worse than what, with a fairer distribution of society's wealth, current technology would permit? We only have one life to live.

Do we really think it's normal that a majority is forced to struggle under increasing pressure just to maintain its standard of living, while a few crisscross the oceans in ever more luxurious yachts? Why do we accept the fact that in spite of universal suffrage time and again a political process prevails which at best serves the interest of the upper 10 percent, and often just the richest 1 percent?

Less competition, more market power

Political decisions are responsible for having altered the face of our economic order in the transition from the twentieth century to the twenty-first—decisions made under the banners of more market, more competition, more freedom, more personal initiative, more growth. Their results are as easily summed up: less market, less competition, more speculation, more dependence and less growth.

Essentially, changes have occurred on three levels in particular. First, a framework of rules for economic life that was created in light of painful earlier crises has been demolished in the name of the free market. The most obvious, though by no means only, example for this is the financial sector. As a consequence, risky business models have multiplied, while the supposedly liberated market was flooded with products that were profitable simply because the finance industries were allowed to externalize most of their cost. In the financial sector, this applies to almost all forms of investment banking, to most so-called derivatives, and high frequency trade. It applies equally to the business idea of corporate raids and bankruptcy speculators, or to global tax savings models through which Amazon, Ikea, etc., unlike smaller firms, dodge their obligations to society. All the cunning tricks and techniques that those at the top of the wealth pyramid use successfully to evade taxes would not work without preceding deregulation and the removal of capital controls.

Among the burdensome rules that were eliminated during the waves of deregulation were anti-trust laws, to the extent that they had retained any authority to curtail economic power in the first place. As a result of all this, from the world of banking to the digital economy, giant global corporations dominating markets and societies were set up whose business decisions now determine the course of the global economy. These corporations do not feel committed to anything but shareholder value. On account of their concentrated economic power, they are able to prevail in almost any industry and at the expense of other market participants. Instead of more competitive pressure, decades of deregulation and market euphoria have produced a greater concentration of economic resources in far fewer hands.

Labour protection as market rigidity

The power of a handful of global corporations was increased in the name of the market within their industry and vis-à-vis suppliers and customers. They have become more powerful also vis-à-vis those whose labour power creates their wealth and that of their shareholders. This is the second level where changes have occurred. Laws designed to protect workers and employees from hire-and-fire practices of reckless profiteers were now referred to as "labour market rigidities." When "structural reforms" are discussed in Europe, this is what is at stake. Social benefits, which in many countries were legally regulated as part of a decent wage and once considered to help preserve human dignity in the face of illness, old age, or unemployment, nowadays are seen only as cost factors that put an excessive burden on businesses and need to be minimized.

Former German Social Democratic Chancellor Gerhard Schröder, supported by the Green Party's Joseph Fischer, as well as current Christian Democratic Chancellor Angela Merkel, in this sense did create a *New Middle Class*. Thanks to the reforms of "Agenda 2010", employees who in the past worked in regular full-time jobs with decent wages and belonged to the middle class, nowadays work as temporary workers, contract workers, pseudo self-employed, limited term workers or part-time. Often their incomes have been cut in half in jobs with uncertain prospects; such workers are found in logistics, on the assembly line at BMW, as cashiers in a drug store chain, or at home in front of a computer. Part of the experience of the *New Middle Class* is the fear of being fired in case of illness or of having to deal with large expenses, as well as the prospect of not receiving a sufficient pension after a long working life. Instead of boosting personal initiative and freedom, this is resulting in dependency and disenfranchisement.

New playgrounds for profiteers

The third level of so-called market orientation has affected areas previously served by public welfare organizations and the government that have become playgrounds for private profiteers. This trend started in housing, the postal service, telecommunications, energy supply, and the railways. It was subsequently extended to formerly municipal utilities such as water works, local transport and garbage removal, and finally reached schools, universities, care facilities, and hospitals. In most of these areas there is not, and cannot be, any real competition. As a result, no new markets were created. Instead, welfare agencies and public suppliers who had not exploited their monopoly position for profit maximization were merely replaced by those whose primary goal is precisely that.

The revenue of the affected enterprises has tended to develop in two directions: steeply upward for management, significantly downward for employees. No one with a minimum of social conscience would find even barely acceptable the principle that those who pay the most are entitled to receive the best product when we are dealing with basic services such as health care, education, or housing. Privatization has contributed to increasing inequality and social polarization in many ways, without creating more competition or strengthening the market.

Twenty-first century economic feudalism

The distribution of wealth and power in today's capitalism, even if at a much higher level of productivity and prosperity, resembles the period when Louis XV and Madame de Pompadour celebrated their lavish parties. As was the case in the Middle Ages, in the eighteenth century about 1 percent of the population belonged to the upper class. They owned the then important economic resources of arable land, grazing grounds, and forests. They dominated public life, jurisprudence, and the application of law. It goes without saying that they did not pay any taxes. The remaining 99 percent of the population directly or indirectly worked for the richest 1 percent. Assets along with the corresponding social status were passed on from one generation to the next according to the principle of inheritance based on blood relation. The son of a peasant became a peasant; the son of a baron became a baron unless he decided in favour of a career in the clergy or in the military, which would allow him to remain in the upper class.

At the start of the twenty-first century, the richest 1 percent control the most important economic resources, with the difference that in addition to agricultural land and real estate, these include industrial facilities, technological know-how, digital and other networks, servers, software, patents, and much more. Ownership of these resources continues to be passed on unchanged from one generation to the next by inheritance. Nowadays, the transfer of these assets is in many cases virtually tax-free, affording a lifestyle far exceeding any working income. Once again, 99 percent of the population for the most part work, directly or indirectly, for the wealth of this new financial aristocracy.

One might object that the decisive difference consists in the fact that, in the feudal era as well as in the period of absolutism, the economy progressed very little since there were few incentives to increase productivity and improve production methods. In contrast, it might be argued that capitalism has created today's enormous wealth, which lifts the life of even the poorest inhabitants of industrialized states way above the level of their ancestors in previous centuries. This is correct as far as the past is concerned. But is it true for the present and the future? Admittedly, production continues to be transformed, digitalization promises enormous productivity increases, new processes are introduced, and new products appear on the market. But who benefits from a dynamic economy if the economic dynamic for the majority points downward? And how innovative is our economy really?

"This economy kills"

Outside the global centres of wealth, the situation is almost hopeless. On our prosperous planet, which thanks to today's technological potential could feed a world population of 12 billion, one billion people suffer from malnutrition and another one billion are starving. The UN warns that in the coming 15 years another 70 million children will die from preventable or treatable poverty-related diseases before reaching the age of 5. 70 million human beings whose lives will be extinguished before they really had a chance to start it, simply because their fate is of no interest to the most powerful political decision-makers and their economic allies. Incidentally, these are the same people who like to justify their wars with the hypocritical claim of protecting human lives and human rights and with the argument that we can't just stand by and watch as people are dying. Yet according to Jacques Diouf, General Secretary of the UN Organization for Food and Agriculture, it would take no more than 30 billion dollars per year in order to end hunger and malnutrition globally—a small fraction of the funds spent on militarization and wars.

The UN has issued many warnings, but little has changed, and change that did occur was often for the worse. Poor countries were forced to sign so-called "free trade agreements", which destroyed their domestic production and opened their markets to Western agricultural and industrial corporations. Millions of small farmers and businesses were wiped out in this way. When in despair people try to make their way to the wealthy countries, they are dismissed as economic refugees. Yet our economy and our corporations are the ones destroying their economic existence and driving them to migrate.

"This economy kills", Pope Francis has reminded the Church and the world. Evidence to back up this statement can be found every day in the countries of the so-called Third World, parts of the world that have been abandoned by the First World. It is true that in earlier centuries people died of hunger when there were extreme droughts or when other natural disasters destroyed crops. But that in a world of plenty in which a significant part of food is not even consumed but thrown out, year after year millions of people should die a cruel death because they have no food—this is a perversion generated by the capitalist world order.

Ruled by organized money

One question is becoming increasingly urgent: do we still need capitalism today in order to have a better life in the future? Or isn't it precisely this form of economic life that keeps us from improving our lives? Do we need the profit motive as an incentive to improve our technologies, so that production stops destroying our planet and with it our basis for survival, or is it the profit-oriented logic of growth itself that ties our hands? What would a better alternative look like? What economic structures are needed for turning good ideas into good products quickly? Where do the incentives to develop new production methods come from—methods that can really move us forward since they will not require us to run our economies by progressively exhausting our natural environment? How can we take advantage of the productivity-enhancing effect of digitalization and industry 4.0 without at the same time generating additional unemployment? How can we achieve a dynamic of innovation that increases not only the wealth of corporations and their owners but of everyone?

Surprisingly, it is not that difficult. We simply have to overcome the economic feudalism of the twenty-first century. Markets should not be abolished but, on the contrary, need to be saved from capitalism. We need what neoliberals claim to achieve but in reality systematically destroy: freedom, individual initiative, competition, performance-based pay, protection of property of one's own creation. Whoever is in favour of change and is serious about it has to end rather than uphold a situation in which the important economic resources and wealth are owned by a tiny upper class that automatically benefits from any additional profit. An upper class that has the power to decide on investments and jobs, and with its major influence on the media, with its think tanks and lobbyists, with its ability to launch campaigns, and with its enormous capital can dominate or buy any government in the world. "Government by organized money is just as dangerous as Government by organized mob"[2], President Roosevelt cautioned in a speech as early as 1936.

What socially useful things do the billions of dollars pay for that in the form of dividends and other gains end up in the pockets of the top 1 percent? And even more important, on what grounds can they claim decision-making power over ever-expanding economic wealth and thus over the development of society as a whole—a privilege they enjoy on account of current property law? The standard justification for capital returns is supposed to be the risk that capital owners take when they make investments.

Limited liability, unlimited profit

How great is this risk really? Limited liability for capital invested in the economy is one of capitalism's original contributions to property rights. In almost all large firms today, liability in case of bankruptcy is limited to no more than the capital initially invested.

And how great is the risk of bankruptcy in established markets dominated by a few large firms? Bankruptcies do occur, as was recently the case with two German retail giants, Karstadt and Schlecker. However, these cases were ruinous mainly for the former employees who lost their jobs rather than for the former owners who lost some of their assets. But is the risk of being demoted from billionaire to millionaire sufficient justification to keep collecting exorbitant incomes? Or is the real threat for a market economy and a democracy that a firm's assets, created by the work of tens of thousands of employees, end up automatically in the bank accounts of capital owners?

What is more, large firms in particular have perfected the art of shifting risks onto others. In the financial sector, the gap between private profit and public liability for losses became all too evident in the banking crisis of 2008. Subsequent cosmetic corrections in banking regulations have not changed the situation. Yet in the real economy government is also regularly called upon to intervene when it comes to risks: tax incentives, different forms of subsidies, and other kinds of public support for the private sector are always gladly accepted. In the end it is tax-financed innovations that make private enterprises rich. Google, Apple, and the entire pharmaceutical industry are prime examples.

Limited liability, automatic transfer of newly created assets to capital owners, and transfer of losses and risks to the state are the main driving forces behind the growing inequality in property distribution and ownership.

Government funds finance private property

True, we would not be better off but significantly poorer if the government were to remove itself completely from economic life. If all struggling banks in 2008 had been left to slide into uncontrolled bankruptcy, the effects on the supply of credit to the economy would have been even more dramatic than they were, and deposit insurance would not have protected the accounts of small savers from losses. If the government were to eliminate all subsidies for research, the process of innovation would slow down even further than it already has in many sectors. Without start-up financing through public risk capital, many firms that enrich our lives with good and useful products would not exist.

The point is not to stop providing any and all economic subsidies. Rather, the point is to eliminate the absurdity that public funds are transformed into private property rights, which are subsequently protected by law even if they turn against public interests. The goal should be an economy that does in fact reward talent and performance, and that enables individuals with ideas, motivation, and business sense to set up firms even if they do not happen to be blessed with a large inheritance. Creative ideas and new technologies that have potential deserve reliable financing that assumes the initial risk and thus access to credit.

At the heart of the power of the upper ten thousand and the origin of their ability to collect incomes without making any contribution is the current constitution of economic property. Transforming economic property structures is therefore the key to a new approach.

Reform proposals that omit this dimension may bring about improvements in certain areas. But in most cases they will end up the way various attempts at banking regulation have: diluted, declawed, and evaded.

Technocratic swamp

In part this is a result of the power disparity between territorially circumscribed state authority and the global scope of economic actors. It is widely believed that democracy could be reinstated if political decision-makers followed the economy's lead in globalizing or Europeanizing. However, this assumption is naive. Democracy can live only in spaces that people can grasp. Only under such conditions does the *demos* have a chance to come into contact with, monitor, and control political decision-makers. The larger, less homogeneous, and complex a political unit, the less the likelihood that democracy will work. If in addition there are different languages and cultures, the project becomes hopeless.

There are good reasons why democracy and the welfare state are the result of struggles in individual nation-states. These institutions are compromised, however, when parliaments and national governments lose power. It is no accident that the institutions of the European Union (EU) in Brussels, which have degenerated into the infamous technocratic swamp lacking transparency and which, more than any national government, are controlled by corporate lobbyists, have completely lost the confidence of a large majority of Europeans. Most of these institutions were set up from the start to function without the need for democratic legitimation. Yet even in the elections to the European Parliament, which occur every five years, barely a third of citizens participate, significantly fewer than in any national parliamentary elections.

The limited authority of the European Parliament is not even the primary reason for this. On the contrary, its decision-making powers have been considerably expanded over the years, while at the same time its democratic legitimation has diminished as a result of constantly declining voter turnout. The main reason for this lack of interest seems to be the fact that the EU Parliament is simply too distant, removed from the experience and lived reality of the populations in the individual countries. As a result, people find it difficult to recognize any of the existing parliamentary alliances composed of heterogeneous parties as their voice and personal interest representation. At least at the national level, members of Parliament have a local constituency where citizens can approach them. But no one knows who "their" representatives in the European Parliament are because they don't exist. This is also why in the German national parliament, the Bundestag in Berlin, there are eight lobbyists for every elected representative, while in Brussels the ratio is twenty to one. Where democratic control fails, the swamp of corruption and the practice of politicians for sale flourishes. Needless to say, this will be reflected in the political agenda.

Re-democratization of states

For the foreseeable future, there is really only one framework in which real democracy can live and which needs to be *re-democratized,* i.e. the historically evolved state with its various sub-levels, from cities and communities to regions and federal units to national parliaments and governments.

Of course it would be desirable and make sense if the European countries were to follow common rules in certain areas, from the environment and consumer protection to corporate taxes. In order to achieve agreement on such issues, we do not need an arrogant European Commission to get involved in what are the sovereign rights of states, and certainly no high-handed president of the European Central Bank to interfere with the government of individual countries. All that would be needed is European-level coordination between elected governments. We should keep in mind that despite the "pooling of sovereignty", the EU has not created adequate rules for dealing with the most important issues. While member states continue to compete with each other over who offers the lowest corporate and wealth tax rates, Brussels dictates budget rules and requires states to let international corporations compete in the provision of public services.

Hayek's European Project

The neoliberal founding father Friedrich von Hayek was convinced that European treaties and institutions could be useful levers for committing policymakers in individual countries to a pro-corporate agenda regardless of election results. For this reason he was a strong proponent of the idea of a European federal state that would be above individual European states—not in order to extend the scope of policymaking, but rather to *undercut* political intervention and thus obstruct democracy.

Hayek is correct when he writes: "the abrogation of national sovereignties and the creation of an effective international order of law is a necessary complement and the logical consummation of the liberal program. [Since ...] on the whole, it is likely that in a federation the weakening of the economic powers of the individual states would and should gradually be carried much further than will at first be evident."[3] Without attracting much attention, a framework could thus be created in which policy makers no longer need to pursue any agenda other than lowering corporate and capital taxes, reduce workers rights and cut public spending, that is to say, follow faithfully Hayek's idea of a *liberal program*. In the end, such a straitjacket would deprive governments of the power to unilaterally maintain "even such legislation as the restriction of child labor or of working hours"[4], as Hayek notes approvingly.

Like the pseudo-Europeans of our time who advocate a reduction of the sovereign rights of states, Hayek was not interested in the European idea or European values. One important European value is after all democracy, which is undermined by European treaties and institutions. In this sense the European Union may well be seen as an *anti-European* project. Since the signing of the Maastricht Treaty in 1992, the EU's central goal has been to immunize policies in individual countries against unpredictable electoral outcomes. In a *market-conforming democracy*, decision-making power lies with the corporations rather than the *demos*.

De-democratization as a result of lost sovereignty

As Hayek knew, in Europe this has become difficult to accomplish at the level of individual states. Notwithstanding pervasive corruption and the power of money, European states continue to have democratic institutions. Parliaments and in some countries the chief executive are periodically elected directly, giving the population the opportunity to toss out corrupt politicians and unpopular parties. This democratic right loses its significance if the population does not have an opportunity to chose a different government agenda, in other words if governments regardless of which parties are in power are no longer able to make sovereign policy choices. The safest way to eliminate this sovereignty is by establishing transnational treaties and institutions that govern democratic states and have to be respected by them. If Hayek were still around to see the European Union of our time, he probably would have been very pleased. His program of *de-democratizing* Europe is far advanced. It would be complete with the adoption and ratification of treaties like CETA and TTIP, which would eliminate any political room for manoeuvre.

If we want to live once again in truly democratic polities, we have to head in the opposite direction. Rather than internationalizing politics, economic structures should be decentralized and shrunk. We need global exchange and trade, but we don't need modern robber barons who organize production on three or four different continents, opting for the places with the cheapest wages and lowest taxes. John Maynard Keynes, Hayek's old opponent, was convinced that "ideas, art, knowledge, hospitality and travel should be international. In contrast, goods should be produced locally wherever it is reasonably possible; above all, however, finance should remain largely in the national context."[5]

Abolishing global capitalism instead of regulating it

Moving to a smaller scale is also necessary for reasons of the economy's efficiency and capacity for innovation. The economic giants with their enormous market power are destroying not only democratic authority, but also genuine competition. There is nothing wrong with firms cooperating on certain projects. But it is a political scandal for a considerable part of European automobile or pharmaceutical production to be interlinked at the level of ownership, or for one British supplier to have most of Europe's communication services under its control. It is equally nonsensical for a German company to run Greek airports or for a Swedish corporation to be in charge of energy supply for German cities and municipalities.

The global capitalism of our time can no longer be domesticated at a national level. Democratically legitimated European or international institutions with this kind of power do not and probably cannot exist. If we really want a better life, modest and minor reforms will not do. The challenge is to save our democracy and market economy from capitalism by embarking on the design of a new economic order.

PART I

PERFORMANCE, INDIVIDUAL RESPONSIBILITY AND COMPETITION: THE GRAND ILLUSIONS OF CAPITALISM

1. THE ROGUE ECONOMY: IS GREED A VIRTUE?

Do we need to be saved from capitalism? May God save us instead from daydreamers, utopians, and naive believers in human goodness who don't understand, or don't want to accept, human nature and its true motivations and causes. With all their magnanimity and good intentions, they would create a catastrophe if ever they were to achieve the power to put their ideas into practice.—Most of us have encountered this notion so frequently in our lives, in any of its many variations, for the automatic response to be triggered. Capitalism, according to this commonsense view, means a dynamic economy, growth, and prosperity because it rewards performance and effort, promising a career and success to those who keep fighting, tolerate adversity, and are persistent in pursuing their goals.

What is bad about an economy that promotes initiative and personal responsibility, but at the same time appeals to ambition, greed, and egoism in order to set free the inexhaustible source of human creativity? True, capitalism does produce great inequality. But is that not precisely the secret recipe motivating people to reach the highest levels of performance—the chance to achieve unimaginable wealth while simultaneously living with the constant risk of social decline?

Humans after all are not noble, helpful, and good. This is why a successful economic system has to start with those characteristics that are typically human instead of relying on those that a majority of people simply do not possess. Sounds plausible. But is this in fact an accurate picture of human nature? An acquisitive, calculating, selfish *homo oeconomicus* whose universe revolves exclusively around himself? This view is immediately contradicted by the fact that loneliness and social isolation cause humans the worst suffering. Even great wealth can usually not make up for this. The connection between wealth and happiness is that the rich experience social exclusion much more rarely and receive more social respect than the poor, usually regardless of the source of their wealth.

Freedom without friends?

It is interesting that in Indo-Germanic languages, the word *freedom* has the same root, *fri*, as the words *friend* and the German word for peace, *Frieden*. *fri* means "to love" and to be free originally meant "to belong to friends" or also "to live in peace (*Frieden*) with others."[6] Not the absence of ties but having ties with others makes you free, because only ties can sustain you. Humans are social creatures who live much more contentedly if they are connected to others than if they feel left alone. Not even capitalism would work if it was populated for the most part by selfish *homines oeconomici* who always calculate how their personal benefit can be maximized. If this image of human nature corresponded to reality, there would be no volunteer work, no citizens' initiatives, no voluntary firefighters, and no associations except for those that could offer material benefits to their members. Ultimately, no school, hospital, or even commercial enterprise would function if everyone contributed only the bare minimum of what their employment contracts stipulate and can be controlled by their bosses. "Work to rule" is not a normal situation, but an implicit rebellion, which would quickly undermine the functioning of any organization.

This is not contradicted by the fact that people will often behave egotistically and that the needs of one's own family are closer and more important than those of strangers. Biological and cultural evolution have equipped us with both: the instinct for self-preservation, which is primarily about one's own and one's family's wellbeing, as well as empathy for the fate of others, ruthlessness and benevolence, resentment and support, greed and the joy of sharing, envy and indignation in the face of injustice even if it happens to others. As individuals, we may all have our own mix of character traits. But what characteristics become dominant in society, what types of behaviour shape a society, depends on what kind of behaviour a society promotes and rewards and what it sanctions by withholding respect and success.

Inequality destroys trust

Results of experimental economics suggest that initially people tend towards cooperative behaviour, which is lost when others respond repeatedly with uncooperative behaviour and make cooperation costly. A child that learns early in life that trust and openness will be exploited and abused by others will become distrustful and withdrawn. In a comparative time-series analysis, British social scientists Richard Wilkinson and Kate Pickett have studied to what extent mutual trust is dependent on social factors. Their findings are clear: The greater the degree of social inequality, the less trust people have in each other. While in the 1960s, 60 percent of Americans had basic trust in their fellow citizens, today this figure is less than 40 percent.[7]

When social cohesion dissolves, being trusting is no longer beneficial but instead increases the risk of being exploited. Wilkinson and Pickett's studies also show that people have measurably less interest and concern for each other when the income gap widens.[8] Thus empathy and solidarity can be socially encouraged or discouraged.

Not property but status

It is really not difficult to comprehend: Where honest people are taken advantage of, lying will be a recipe for success. But does it follow that people are born liars? Where the unselfish are for the most part exploited, selfishness and a chilly social climate will thrive. Yet do we not feel better in a social environment of a different kind?

As the economic historian Karl Polanyi emphasized, people's goals are always embedded in social relations. He writes: "He does not act so as to safeguard his individual interest in the possession of material goods; he acts so as to safeguard his social standing, his social claims, his social assets."[9] This is supported by the fact that as a rule people view their material situation in relation to that of others. When behavioural experiments ask whether the subject would prefer having a monthly income of 4000 euros in a society where the average income is 2000 euros, or a monthly income of 5000 euros in a wealthy society where the average income is 10,000 euros, a majority will regularly opt for the lower income of 4000.

God-given greed

Since people are social creatures, they greatly care about what others think of them. Socially prohibited behaviour is therefore avoided, at least to the extent that this is an option. Of course social disapproval of begging and stealing will not keep a poor person lacking any opportunity for work or other support from doing either. However, the religious prohibition of commercial activity made it more difficult for the Catholic nobility in France and Spain to ruthlessly increase their wealth through early capitalist methods than for their Calvinist and Puritan counterparts in the Netherlands or England.

Religious and social legitimation of characteristics previously considered as a vice such as monetary greed, selfishness, and lack of social concern were at least as important for the ascent of capitalism as was the invention of the steam engine. Calvinism, for example, glorified ruthless self-enrichment as a God-given virtue. According to the Calvinist moral canon, failing to take advantage of a profit opportunity was a graver abdication of religious duty than showing a lack of concern for others. A community in which a majority of members is guided by such a morality is necessarily a cold, brutal, and unfriendly place.

Mandeville's Fable of the Bees

In non-religious spheres, the legitimation of unscrupulousness and villainy was also advanced with fervour. Even before Adam Smith—and much more radically and cynically—the Anglo-Dutch physician and writer Bernard Mandeville praised the social benefit of greed and selfishness. His bestseller, *The Fable of the Bees*, first appeared in 1714 with the subtitle "Private Vices—Public Benefits". The story is about a beehive that is rich, powerful, respected, and successful, even though—or precisely because—it provides an environment in which fraud, lies, and crime thrive. Everything is working just fine—the rich bees bathe in luxury and live out their greedy lust for ever-increasing wealth without restraint while the poor bees slave away producing the luxury goods for the rich bees, which does at least give them work and an income. Of course, morality or fairness of course have no role to play.

The life of the prosperous community, however, is interrupted by the God Jupiter, who shows up uninvited and severely reprimands the sinful bees in order to return them to a virtuous life. Enrichment is now prohibited, and the rich bees henceforth live modestly and are content with life's basic necessities. As a result, the crafts and trades are ruined, the entire bee hive becomes impoverished, while the poor bees are much worse off than they were before since they can't find any work. The conclusion happens to be precisely the moral with which we are all too familiar.

In the cynical view of Mandeville, the rich ought to be proud of their extravagant lifestyle, since it creates opportunities for the poor to earn their keep. Few would nowadays put it so bluntly, but in a somewhat more subtle form we encounter this argument to this day.

False philanthropists and respectable fraudsters

It is quite common for the super-rich to exert massive pressure in order to push their investments towards maximum returns, exploiting any legal loopholes they can find in order to minimize their tax payments. At the same time, they boost their reputation by engaging in philanthropic projects which tend to cost them only a fraction of the taxes they have evaded, while all the more effectively burnishing their personal image. In her book on the super-rich, Canadian writer Chrystia Freeland quotes a billionaire who describes the way the super-rich view themselves in the following words: "It is the top one percent that probably make bigger contributions towards the betterment of the world than the remaining 99 percent. I've never seen any poor people do what Bill Gates has done. I've never seen poor people hire a lot of other people. That's why I believe we should honour and hold up the one percent, those who have created value."[10] The question by what means and at whose expense someone like Bill Gates has made his billions in the first place is usually not discussed in such views.

How the top one percent view themselves is one thing. As long as the rest of us adopt greed and selfishness as the basis of society's wealth, as long as we do not look down upon the unrestrained enrichment on the part of those who are already wealthy but instead shower them with admiration, we give all the greedy and selfish people the pleasant feeling of being socially accepted. And then we are surprised if highly profitable corporations do not have the slightest compunction about developing ever more sophisticated models for how to lower wages, circumvent environmental laws, or defraud society of the last cent of taxes they owe, all for the sake of achieving another half percent of additional profit. Or investment bankers with their bets on derivatives, which may double the price of corn or undermine entire states, doing so without even the slightest scruples and with a great deal of self-satisfaction.

Repulsive people with repulsive motives

Humans are not by nature ruthless, greedy, and selfish. However, a society that provides the greatest opportunities to the selfish, the greedy, and the ruthless and considers them smart, whereas allegedly good people are seen as simple-minded and naive, should not expect the majority of its members to act in the spirit of fairness and solidarity. What is perhaps more surprising is how many people nevertheless continue acting in this way.

Keynes once remarked that capitalism was based on "the peculiar conviction that repulsive people with repulsive motives would somehow produce general welfare." One might argue that for a certain period of time this approach did more or less work. By now, however, it would be difficult to find in the actions of "repulsive people" and their "repulsive motives" any positive contribution to our common good. How could one object to the idea that in the future we should try out an economic order in which decent people with respectable motives promote the common good?

2. RISE AND DECLINE: HOW INNOVATIVE IS OUR ECONOMY?

Perhaps the critics of capitalism ought to look back on the unprecedented economic dynamic of the past two centuries. Has this record not demonstrated beyond doubt that, notwithstanding certain dark sides, Adam Smith's "invisible hand" in the long run has functioned well—by establishing property rights, competition and free entrepreneurship, which channel people's selfishness in a positive direction for society as a whole? There may be good reasons for a degree of redistribution, the alleviation of poverty, and the taxation of wealth. But transcend capitalism? Wouldn't that be like throwing out the highly talented baby with the bathwater?

Fairy tales

At first glance, capitalism's record is indeed impressive. For our ancestors, accustomed to economic stagnation and at best minor innovations, it would sound like a fairy tale. Between 1700 and 2012, global per-capita income multiplied tenfold while world population, for centuries remaining below 1 billion, grew a factor of six. In the industrialized countries, the real income per person is more than twenty times what it was in the early eighteenth century. No one can deny that these numbers represent a significant improvement in the quality of life, even for the poorer section of the population. Compared to our ancestors in previous centuries, we live much longer lives and rarely have to see our children die. On average we work less, have a more diverse diet, are more mobile, are able to easily communicate with each other over long distances and can cure diseases that for thousands of years spelled certain death.

There is no other period in human history during which our capacity to produce material wealth would have increased so rapidly. Never before were technologies of production revolutionized in such a rapid and fundamental way. "The worlds of Goethe and Plato had more similarities with each other than the worlds of Goethe and people living today", Walter Eucken, father of the ordoliberal Freiburg School of Economics, wrote at the beginning of his treatise on *The Principles of Economic Policy*. It is evident that this transformation was a result of the economic order emerging with the Industrial Revolution—or thanks to which an industrial revolution might have happened in the first place.

Fetid sewers

Upon further inspection, however, the picture becomes more nuanced. The capitalist era was certainly not an age of continuously growing mass prosperity, especially on a global scale, and not even in the richest countries. Periods of growth are always followed by periods in which past gains in the standard of living are lost. A bustling economy combined with growing poverty is not a new experience. In fact, this cocktail is typical for the entire first century of capitalism's march to victory. The hellish factories of Manchester and Liverpool with their cruel labour conditions, their putrid air, poison-laced sewage, and absence of hygienic infrastructure forced upon the workers of that time more suffering and a significantly shorter life than that of their rural ancestors. Marx and Engels described this misery in vivid terms. After visiting Manchester, even the liberal Alexis de Toqueville recalled a "fetid sewer", a "dirty pool", in which "civilized people are returned to the beasts."[11]

Even though capitalist industrialization in the nineteenth century produced an unprecedented increase in productivity and wealth, wages stagnated until the 1880s at a level so miserably low that physical degeneration ensued. This became evident, for example, in the ranks of the army. Between 1830 and 1860, the average height of English soldiers decreased by two centimetres, while their general state of health became measurably poorer, as the British military administration noted with some concern. Child mortality reached frightening proportions in all of Europe's larger industrial cities. Not until 1880 did the wage level noticeably increase in England as well as on the continent. This period of an improving standard of living for the working population came to an end with the outbreak of World War I.

A conservative party in favour of a shared economy

In the subsequent three decades, two world wars and a global economic crisis disrupted the economy to such an extent that the view that capitalism had become outdated was widely held among sectors of the population that traditionally had few sympathies for the ideas of the Left. In its 1947 program, the conservative German political party CDU (Christian Democratic Union) called for a non-private "shared economic order" instead of capitalism, since "the capitalist economic system has failed to live up to the political and social interests of the German people."

It was not until the New Deal in the United States and the new social model in post-World War II Europe—which we tend to assume is the normal state of capitalism—that a period of rapid economic growth and increasing mass consumption started. For the first time the personal wealth curve pointed upward for all sectors of the population. Inequality as well as poverty declined, a broad middle class emerged, and for several decades it seemed there were no limits to production and consumption. However, this "golden period" is now history.

What is our current situation? Does capitalism continue to be as dynamic and innovative as its advocates would have us believe?

The urgent problems on the agenda today should be indisputable. A minimum goal is a global end to hunger. We need to solve the energy problem by drastically reducing CO_2 emissions while avoiding other dangerous side effects and environmental destruction. We need mobility without particulate and noise pollution, a recycling economy instead of disposable products, early detection, healing and prevention of cancers and other serious diseases. Even more important would be to disable the economic driving forces behind wars and civil wars, which destroy the lives and livelihoods of millions of people. On all these issues of existential importance we have hardly made any progress over the past thirty years—in some respects we've even regressed.

"I'm missing the future. Nowadays we have such low expectations for the future"[12], says internet pioneer and computer scientist Jaron Lanier. The founder of the digital financial service provider PayPal and Internet billionaire Peter Thiel holds a similar view: "The smartphones that distract us from our surroundings also distract us from the fact that our surroundings are strangely old: only computers and communications have improved dramatically since midcentury."[13]

Dead end street instead of innovation

In many sectors we have reached dead ends. Our economy still largely rests on the combustion engine invented in the nineteenth century, even though its damaging effects on health, the climate, and the environment have long been known. Instead of research into minimizing poisonous emissions, Volkswagen and others prefer to invest in sophisticated software to dupe testing agencies. While electric cars are being produced, demand for them is weak, which is hardly surprising in light of their high cost and an underdeveloped infrastructure. And even the electric motor will not represent significant progress as long as we use primarily fossil fuels to produce our energy.

Why is it that alternatives to fossil fuels continue to be so underdeveloped? In only 88 minutes, the sun radiates 470 exajoule on the earth, equivalent to humanity's energy consumption for a whole year. If we were able to capture just one-tenth of one percent of solar energy, this would yield six times the amount of energy the world economy needs today. But we are not moving forward. Solar cells are nowadays better than they were 20 years ago, but far from sufficient to solve the energy problem in countries of the north. Solar manufacturers are under pressure, many have gone bankrupt, and there is no room for large research budgets.

Eco-gamblers enriched

Wind power as well represents a huge potential source of energy. According to a Stanford University study, capturing 20 percent of wind power would be sufficient to produce the electricity that the world economy currently consumes. Nevertheless, we keep burning oil and coal. While enormous steel structures for wind turbines have come to dominate the landscape in Germany, they are not properly integrated into its energy grid. When the wind blows, the country gives away excess electricity to its neighbours, when it doesn't, the oldest coal-fired power plants are reactivated because modern gas power plants are not economically competitive in this constellation.

We send space probes to Mars while the necessary storage capacity for green electricity is not available or extremely expensive—a clear sign for insufficient research activity and an absence of pressure for innovation. The particular energy mix in Germany today emits more CO_2 into the atmosphere than was the case before the "green" energy revolution. Since the year 2000, increasing electricity prices have subsidized this foolishness with well over 100 billion euros. Instead of promoting the development of Green technologies, state subsidies have enriched eco-gamblers and landowners that lease land to the operators of wind turbines.

Keynes imagining the year 2028

Consider how quickly, in the nineteenth century steam, power was replaced by electricity, how rapidly in the twentieth century assembly line production and later automatization were phased in, and the speed at which digitalization is advancing. Reading Keynes's beautiful short essay on the "Economic Possibilities for our Grandchildren" published in 1928, you realize what hopes for the future even such sober analysts as Keynes harboured in view of the technological breakthroughs of the time.

Keynes firmly assumed that within a period of 100 years, humanity would have solved "its economic problem". He anticipated that by the year 2028, all essential needs would be satisfied while working time would have been reduced to at most three hours per day. As he wrote optimistically, "for the first time since his creation man will be faced with his real, his permanent problem—how to use his freedom from pressing economic cares, how to occupy the leisure which science and compound interest will have won for him, to live wisely and agreeably and well." [...] "The love of money as a possession—as distinguished from the love of money as a means to the enjoyments and realities of life—will be recognised for what it is, a somewhat disgusting morbidity, one of those semi-criminal, semi-pathological propensities which one hands over with a shudder to the specialists in mental disease."[14]

How incredibly distant we seem to be from this future! Silicon Valley is considered the world's most innovative workshop for ideas, but where are the ideas that can help us make progress on our truly most pressing problems? And where in Europe are such ideas developed? True, the computer and the Internet have revolutionized our lives, but even those two inventions originated in the middle of the last century and were widely adopted by the 1990s.

Uber and Ryanair

Where are the revolutionary inventions and innovations of the early twenty-first century? Is it the smartphone, which, for marketing purposes, appears each year in a new version without offering anything truly new? Is it the search engine Google, which has become an insatiable data monster that gobbles up everything it can about us? Or is it the various social networks that collect our most private feelings, analyze them, and commercialize them? Is that what the world has been waiting for? Or is it perhaps the latest app from Uber, which has the potential power to destroy the existing taxi industry, getting us more cheaply to our destination, except that our driver will have no retirement or health plan, and an even lower income than cab drivers do today?

Our airplanes are not flying any faster or with fewer emissions than they were 20 years ago. The only significant "innovation" in this sector has been the introduction of low-cost airlines with poorly paid crews, minimal service, and cramped seats. Low-income earners may now find some flights more affordable for themselves—if they book well in advance, sacrifice flexibility and travel with cabin luggage only. This innovation means that both the flight attendant and the pilot have to worry about their next rent increase. Is that really what we mean by progress?

Fat and salty

Our industrially manufactured foods are for the most part unhealthy: too much fat, salt, and sugar. This is the case despite the fact that we have far greater knowledge about nutrition than only two or three decades ago. Some things have become cheaper over the past few years, but a lot of things are now of lower quality. There are food scandals all the time because of ingredients that make people sick and shouldn't be in there in the first place. This almost always happens for reasons of pathological cost-cutting or dumping. International treaties such as TTIP and CETA threaten to undermine hard-fought environmental and consumer protection standards.

There may well be innovative ideas in many research labs. But those that actually make it to market include fracking, which poisons the soil in the process of extraction; genetically modified food, the long-term consequences of which for the environment and health are not known; genetically modified seeds that increase hunger and dependency globally; diet pills that cause disease rather than curing it; and potentially addictive Internet games. Even in the centre of Europe nuclear power plants continue to be built as if there was no tomorrow. The main application of rapidly growing digital storage capacity is spying on and recording our private lives—for the purpose of commercial exploitation for advertisers, insurers, creditors, or potential employers, or for the purpose of government surveillance and state security.

Purchased, used, discarded

We're all familiar with these products: cell phones, printers, refrigerators or washing machines that stop working properly once their warranty period expires. The trend is undeniable: appliances we purchase today may be technologically more sophisticated but at the same time break much more quickly than their precursors did twenty or thirty years ago.

Contrary to the requirements of recycling and extended durability, manufacturers intentionally devise products with a short life that are difficult or impossible to repair. Spare parts are either expensive or may not even be produced. This practice is not entirely new. The oldest known instance of manufacturers reducing product quality by design is the Phoebus light bulb cartel of 1924. At that time, the large international manufacturers agreed to reduce the lifespan of light bulbs from the technologically possible 2,500 hours to 1,000 hours in order to boost sales. Nowadays tricks like installing low-quality components that quickly wear down or the use of cheap materials with a short life are even more widespread than they were in the last century, especially in markets dominated by a small number of suppliers. A 2014 study on "planned obsolescence" lists an enormous number of concrete examples of such practices.[15]

On occasion the manipulators are exposed. In the early 2000s, Apple produced iPods with a non-replaceable battery with an apparently intentionally limited lifetime of 18 months. This led to a class action suit, with the corporation eventually agreeing to replace the device. However, in most cases these manipulations are difficult to prove and there is no legal action.

Quick and dirty

The former Vice President of the Technical University of Berlin, Wolfgang Neef, describes the turn from quality production to product dumping in vivid terms. He identifies two opposing approaches that have confronted each other from the beginning of capitalism. One is the approach of "engineers who are dealing with the natural laws of chemistry and physics", the other approach is that of "economists who work according to socially constructed "laws" of the market, competition, and profit as a company's sole criteria of success." As long as both approaches have a place in companies, the first step is product development according to technological necessities, and only then will there be discussion of possible cost reductions. The result is products constructed according to professional principles with a relatively low price.

With the start of the neoliberal radicalization of capitalism since about 1985, Neef notes, this balance has shifted more and more in favour of the economics of cost cutting. "My students tell me that at Siemens [a large German multinational corporation], any time-consuming professional engineering work that does not use the cheapest inputs is vilified as 'over-engineering'. Instead, the main objective should be 'value engineering' which is primarily oriented towards shareholder value and for this reason proceeds according to the precept 'quick and dirty'." He further quotes a top Siemens manager as saying, "don't bother me with technology, I have better things to do."[16]

In such corporations, the development of innovative technologies is championed only if it promises to satisfy high profit expectations. "A Siemens employee reported that a return of 16 percent has become the minimum standard for new product developments. He himself had developed an innovation in the area of renewable energy that would have yielded a 15 percent financial return. It was not approved because it fell short of the expected profit margin."[17]

Anglo-Saxon models

The models for this kind of corporate management originate in the Anglo-Saxon countries. For years, employees of IBM have accused management of driving up profits only by way of acquisitions and sell-offs as well as sophisticated financial manipulations, while investment has dropped off and few innovations are being developed. The German business daily *Handelsblatt* sees this as a general pattern: "Instead of inventing products, US firms massage the numbers ... Instead of hiring scientists, setting up new labs or staking out new business fields, US corporations expand their finance departments." Their main activity consists in developing new tricks for international tax arbitrage in order to increase net profits.[18]

This trend is confirmed by an interdisciplinary MIT study that looked at strengths and weaknesses of the American system of innovation and the reasons for the decline in industrial production. It examined why promising innovations often come to a halt or migrate abroad before they become marketable. According to the study, one of the reasons is that large internal departments of research and development are a thing of the past. Most corporations were no longer engaged in long-term basic research or applied research but rather focused spending on short-term goals. Accordingly, new gaps had developed in the industrial ecosystem.[19] It is no longer only US corporations that act in this way—many large European and German companies have also adopted this model in recent decades.

Inventions contra patents

Modern patent law, at the top-of-the-list of lobbying efforts by large corporations, contributes to paralyzing innovation. A 2003 study by the German Fraunhofer Institute which the authors tellingly published under the title "Inventions contra Patents"[20] examines the discrepancy measurable since the early 1990s between the modest increase in companies' R & D spending and the steep increase in their registration of patents doubling in number between 1990 and 2000. This gap has further widened in subsequent years.

The study concludes that a steadily growing share of patent registrations no longer aims to protect a company's own inventions. Instead, the main goal is to block competitors from applying certain technologies. For this purpose, patenting is done in a much broader fashion than would be necessary for the protection of technological innovation, or processes are patented that are not based on any innovation. Increasingly patents are registered not for exclusive use in production, but rather to *prevent* the use of an innovation that poses a threat to the company's own products.

Blockade instead of protection

According to the above-mentioned study by the Fraunhofer Institute, the lion's share of patent registrations serves the purpose of blocking the use of innovations by competitors. This is the crucial cause of the rapid increase in the number of registered patents. By contrast, in small and medium-size companies, research and patent registrations diverge in the opposite way. According to studies by the European Patent Office, two-thirds of small and medium-sized firms actively involved in research fail to protect their innovations through patents because they are put off by the bureaucracy, costs, and time required.[21]

In addition, a patent is useless if the claims to which it entitles the holder cannot be legally defended internationally. The costs of such patent processes for smaller firms can quickly become ruinous. Accordingly, this sector has a steadily declining share in registered patents and is particularly hard hit by legal action on the part of large corporations with their enormous patent holdings. Unfortunately, no statistics are available that could tell us how many innovative small companies have been ruined as a result of such legal disputes—with all the negative consequences this has for the economy's power to innovate.

According to the findings of the Fraunhofer Institute, particularly in markets with fewer competitors patents are being used today as effective tools to exclude new entrants from a market. Start-ups as a rule do not stand a chance in patent-intensive markets. Citing an engineer in automation technology, Neef confirms that the current patenting practice is paralyzing innovation and lowering quality standards: "Developments need to bypass the patents of competitors, and are therefore suboptimal. This is why we are forced to deal with legal tricks instead of producing good technology."[22]

Thus a realistic survey of economic development over the past few decades demonstrates that even in the richer countries, capitalism is no longer as innovative as it claims to be, and where innovations do take place they serve the common good less and less often.

Depression instead of dynamic growth

In the regions of the world outside the centres of wealth, economic depression is palpable. According to calculations of the World Bank, the average income per person in Africa is lower today than it was at the time the colonial system was dismantled. In many countries that used to have planned economies, the introduction of capitalism precipitated a collapse of economic performance from initial levels that were not particularly high. Mongolia, for instance, lost almost all its industry in this process. In the countries of the western Balkans, current production is 10 percent lower than it was in 1989. Twenty-five years of capitalism have not only failed to produce any growth, but have also resulted in a significant lowering of the standard of living. The same is true for many regions in Russia today.

Of course there are counterexamples of rapidly growing economic powers, such as China or South Korea, which in recent decades have experienced large gains in wealth. But is it capitalism that has made them rich? What is it they do differently from and better than the losers? And on what basis did the industrialized countries enjoy their many years of dynamic economic growth? Is there a chance of returning to this situation? Why has the "invisible hand" stopped working in so many countries? And what is so original about this principle we call *capitalist*? These are questions to be addressed in the coming chapters.

3. DISHWASHER LEGENDS, FEUDAL DYNASTIES, AND THE DISAPPEARING MIDDLE

3.1 Top incomes without work

Human perception is not an empty canvas for representing the external world. We shape what we see, and as a rule we see only what is in accordance with pre-existing patterns in our mind.

These patterns include a view of capitalism as an economic order that follows the rules of the market and competitive performance where anyone who puts in the effort can succeed. Even critics of capitalism have often internalized this logic to such an extent that they present their opposition to inequality as if they were asking for charity: the strong can shoulder more weight than the weak, runs a typical justification for higher taxes for the rich. The *strong*? "Top performers" is a typical phrase when referring to the upper echelons of the income pyramid. Alternatively, there is a call for the strong to show solidarity with the weak. Does this mean that rich equals strong? And the weaker and poorer would then be those who by nature are less talented or who simply don't feel like making an effort?

Men of leisure or men of power

Property is the result of work, as the liberal philosopher John Locke taught us at the dawn of the capitalist age. In this account, extensive property is the result of especially hard work or exceptionally creative work. By generously rewarding the powerful men and women who perform this work, thus advancing the economy, doesn't capitalism ensure that we're all better off in the end?

Whoever shares this view of the world has little reason to consider the current distribution of income and wealth unfair. How could one object to high performers having a better life than the idle who just live for the moment? In this view, the only function of government policy can be to ensure that the differences do not become excessive, thus threatening social stability. A humane approach would entail that every person, even those contributing little or nothing, has a right to have her basic needs covered. However, this also defines the limits of government redistribution: market-based distribution should not be corrected to such an extent that the motivation for personal initiative and willingness to work hard are undermined, thus endangering the crucial engine of economic development.

Performance-enhancing drugs for success?

We're all familiar with these images, many of us follow them in our thinking, often quite unconsciously. They make sense because they appear plausible in the everyday world that surrounds us—a world in the middle of society where most of us live. In this world, we encounter the more intelligent and the more simple-minded, the highly educated and the low-skilled, workaholics and party animals, the serious and the gamblers. Who could deny that these differences between people imply different opportunities for work, income, and wealth? But do these differences even come close to accounting for the enormous gap that exists between the small top of society and the large rest?

Is the distribution of wealth a result of competitive performance in free markets? It would be interesting to know what performance-enhancing drugs the upper ten thousand take that has made it possible for them to accumulate private wealth outstripping the combined wealth of 99 percent of humanity. When we look at the facts, no one would seriously want to defend the thesis that the increasing inequality of incomes and assets in recent years has been the result of increased performance by the few and the growing incompetence of the large majority. What then are the real causes of this growing inequality?

From garage entrepreneur to billionaire?

Let's first have a look at the gap between those at the top and the rest of society. Did the principle ever hold that those who are talented and make an effort can make it to the top—from dishwasher to billionaire, from garage entrepreneur to boss of a global IT corporation? If this were the case, why are there such an astonishingly small number of examples for such careers, and why upon closer inspection do they lose much of their grandeur? Only the smallest number of billionaires ever started out with nothing; most of them had private or public patrons or sponsors.

In the nineteenth century, it was still considered self-evident that success could not be achieved through learning, talent, and effort. Even those who belonged to the middle class knew that they would never achieve the lifestyle of the rich. For a worker, a middle class standard of living as a rule remained an unattainable dream, never mind the luxury of the rich. In his international bestseller *Capital in the Twenty-first Century*, French economist Thomas Piketty points out that during the Belle Époque, the wealthiest 1 percent of Parisian citizens made on average 80–100 times the average wage. For what they received per year for being idle, it would have taken a worker a hundred years of drudgery.

Men of leisure at the top

This has not fundamentally changed in the twentieth and twenty-first centuries. As Piketty writes with respect to the structure of top incomes, supported by data based on tax records and other statistics: "In all countries and in all ages, the further you move up within the top ten percent, the more explicit is the decrease in the share of income from work, while the share of capital income systematically and strongly increases."[23]

The difference between the past and the present is that in the nineteenth century, the wealthiest 1 percent lived almost exclusively from capital income without doing any work, whereas nowadays only the wealthiest among them live in complete idleness. In our economic order, the absolute top incomes go not to the hard working but to the wealthy. Compared to the hundreds of millions euros in dividends taken in annually by BMW heiress Susanne Klatten, BMW workers and even CEOs are paupers. The true men and women of leisure have always been at the very top in capitalism.

This does not mean that the super-rich spend their lives by the poolside in the sun, sipping cocktails brought to them by their servants all day long. It only means that this is what they could do if they wanted to. In reality, the super rich include hard-working, entrepreneurial or otherwise active individuals, some of whom may be personally modest—not just the jet-set whose lifestyle comes pretty close to the stereotype of decadent idlers. But those differences are not what matters here. The point is that, whether idle or hard-working, the millions in income at the top of society's wealth pyramid flow regardless of work or performance.

Max Weber's error

It was Max Weber's still influential error to identify the *spirit* of capitalism with the Protestant work ethic. True, capitalism needs disciplined hard workers, who preferably do not make demands for a better life but are content just to keep doing their jobs. Without such workers, capitalism would have never achieved its enormous growth rates. But they are needed at the bottom and in the middle, not at the top of society. In this respect, capitalism is about as closely related to the ethos of hard work and effort as is late French Absolutism with its nobility celebrating wild parties at the courts of Louis XV and Louis XVI.

In this light, it is hardly surprising that the liberation of capitalism over the past three decades has significantly increased the share of national income accruing to income from wealth without any work, while correspondingly reducing the share of income from employment or self-employment. In 1950, about 83 percent of the pie for distribution went to payment for work performed by employees and the self-employed, while only 17 percent flowed to income from wealth. This rate of distribution remained more or less unchanged until the early 1980s. Subsequently, the share of income from assets without work started to grow strongly, reaching one-third of total national income, i. e. twice as high as it was before 1980.

Firms as investment objects

The term *capitaliste* appeared for the first time in France in 1753. It simply referred to a person who owns assets on the proceeds of which he lives. It is precisely in this sense that the famous Austrian economist Joseph Schumpeter put a great deal of emphasis on the distinction between an entrepreneur and a capitalist. According to Schumpeter, an entrepreneur is someone who works in his firm and who as a rule has established this enterprise himself. With his ideas, inspiration, and power, he is the centre of the enterprise, responsible for its successes and failures, and living on the income from this entrepreneurial activity. It is a very different situation from that of the capitalist who is interested in the enterprise only as an investment object.

As long as an entrepreneur continues to have a personal relationship with his firm and its production, he has not yet become a genuine capitalist. The capitalist is interested not in quality but quantity, he simply wants to get optimal growth for his money. A capitalist is therefore not simply a wealthy individual but someone who derives a large part of his living from the returns on his investments. Much like the old nobility lived on the compulsory labour of its tenants, he lives on the income generated by his capital.

Small capitalists?

Yet aren't most of us recipients of income derived from assets, even if just from a savings account or a retirement savings plan? Except for the poorest, don't we all possess some capital and complain about receiving hardly any interest? This is a standard argument in order to make the holders of small amounts of savings feel like they are in the same boat with those who own billions in assets, such as Bill Gates, Warren Buffet, or the Koch brothers.

This argument has little connection with reality. Interest on savings accounts represents a minimal portion of capital income. This is why the current low-interest rate period has barely affected the growth of this type of income. Even though the average citizen in fact no longer receives any interest on her money, the share of capital income in total national income continues to expand.

One of Piketty's central theses is that the rate of return on an asset is directly related to the size of this asset. In short, the more you invest, the higher your return. It is no secret that with the size of capital holdings, there is a change into what types of investment the capital flows. The financial nobility invests in private hedge funds, shares, derivatives, real estate funds, and natural resources that are not listed on the stock exchange and aren't open to small investors. One might assume that large capital holdings have a higher return in the short term because those investments are more high risk. But this is not the case. The differences in return occur in the long term and consistently, whereas according to conventional theory they should be lower because they would have to make up for higher losses in high-risk investments. Intuitively, this is our common sense view. Every real estate agent will tell you that the return on a condominium relative to the amount invested would be significantly higher if you could afford to buy the whole building.

The Matthew effect again

It is not easy to prove this as a general rule since there are few statistics on the returns made by individual capital owners. Piketty has solved the problem by using publicly accessible data on long-term average returns of capital assets held by American universities. He demonstrates that the returns vary directly with the size of the invested capital. In the period 1980–2010, the highest rates of return, an average 10.2 percent after inflation and costs, were achieved by Harvard, Yale, and Princeton, each with several billion dollars in the capital market. Universities with at least 1 billion dollars in assets achieved a return of 8.8 percent, while universities below 100 million had to content themselves with 6.2 percent. The average savings account holder can only dream of such returns. They must be happy if the real "return" on their money—i.e. interest after inflation and bank charges—is not actually negative.

Piketty summarizes his conclusion as follows: "The higher returns of the largest endowments are not due primarily to greater risk taking but to a more sophisticated investment strategy that consistently produces better results."[24] These results explain why the capital of billionaires has been growing annually by 6–7 percent, more recently even by 8–10 percent, in sharp contrast to the assets of the middle class. The latter are currently melting away due to negative interest rates designed to deal with the public debt crisis. Clearly, assets have to shrink if the goal is to lower the debt, but nowadays only the assets of small investors are being hit.

Different worlds

The fact that interest rates for normal savings are close to zero is quite consistent with the thesis that capital income without work is just as integral a part of capitalism as were feudal rents for princes and dukes in the age of feudalism.

It is in the upper 10 percent of the population that capital incomes contribute significantly to personal wealth. The further we climb up in the income hierarchy, the greater the significance of capital income. However, within the stratum of the wealthiest 10 percent we still find two different worlds. One segment of these 10 percent consists of the high-income self-employed, such as doctors, consultants, and lawyers, the owner-managers of mid-sized enterprises, as well as the top managers and experts in corporations and banks. This group is wealthy and has to work hard for their income—they can pass on to their children only their wealth but not their social status or income.

To this extent this group moves in a completely different world from the actual upper class, the "stratosphere of the '1 percent'"[25], as Piketty calls them, a world they are rarely able to reach in spite of 16-hour days, permanent jetlag, and huge stress. "But within the 1 percent, the awareness of the different tiers of wealth is as keen as an Indian matchmaker's sensitivity to the finer divisions of caste.", writes Cynthia Freeland about her personal experiences with the *Plutocrats*, the super-rich.[26] The stratification has nothing to do with personal life achievements. The road to the truly large incomes, which are based on wealth rather than work, is not one of hard work, intelligence and effort but above all depends on inheritance or marriage.

Gates and Bettencourt

There is also the case of former entrepreneurs who initially worked and established their own enterprises, only subsequently becoming capitalist rentiers living on the work of others. In these—not very frequent—cases, membership in the upper class is not a result of either inheritance or marriage but of setting up a highly successful enterprise. Yet with the growth of the enterprise, the returns become increasingly independent of personal work, to the point where no work at all is necessary.

Piketty mentions the example of Bill Gates, whose wealth increased from 4 billion dollars to 50 billion between 1990 and 2010. Gates's billions grew at the same speed as those of the French heiress to L'Oreal, Liliane Bettencourt, which in the same period grew from 2 billion to 25 billion. Even though Bettencourt has never worked a day in her life, she enjoyed the same growth in her wealth of 13 percent annually. When Gates left his corporation in 2008 to spare himself the pain of gainful work, his wealth kept growing apace. As Piketty concludes: "Once capital assets are in existence, their dynamic follows its own logic, and capital can increase substantially simply on account of its mere existence."[27]

3.2 On the futility of saving as a method of accumulating capital

Capitalism betrays in its name what really matters in order to make it to the very top: capital, not work. But how then to get hold of capital? Those who continue to defend the myth of an economic order based on hard work and personal effort have to make a case for the theory that capital is the result of hard work and a frugal life. An individual who works and saves a lot, or so the story goes, will one day have as much wealth as Gates or Bettencourt. The realism of this story is such that it deserves an honorary place in the fairy tales of the Brothers Grimm, right next to Cinderella.

The assets of the middle class

True, if you work hard, earn a good salary, and regularly save some of it, you may be able to accumulate a fair amount of wealth. If you buy your own home, you will own property based on your own work. The same applies to savings accounts, life insurances, and other financial investments for which those with an above average income are able to set aside part of their salary.

This kind of wealth has reached significant proportions only since the emergence of a large middle class in the second part of the twentieth century. In the nineteenth and early twentieth centuries, the idea that capital was the result of hard work and frugality would have appeared rather strange. Then, as in the more distant past, the existence of personal wealth was a privilege of the wealthiest 10 percent of the population, while 90 percent of all wealth was concentrated in the richest 1 percent. The rest owned nothing, and their low incomes forced them to live from hand to mouth.

For the poorer half of the population in the industrialized countries, this continues to be the case. To be able to save in the first place, you have to earn more than you need to cover basic living costs. The refusal to acknowledge this simple fact is the basis for all private retirement savings plans, which precisely for this reason regularly fail low-income earners.

Money vs capital

The crucial fact is: the middle class does have money and it does own real estate. What it does not possess to any significant extent is capital. And confusing money and capital is one of the major errors that stand in the way of understanding the current economic order.

What is capital? In its simplest version, the concept of "capital" is often just equated with machines, know-how, and buildings—what is referred to as a firm's real capital. In this view, any manufacturing employing machinery would be *capitalist* production. If we don't want to return to the hoe and the horse-drawn plough, there will be no overcoming capitalism. But such a definition is nonsense.

Even individual firms do not actually record their physical capital goods as real capital, but in terms of their monetary value. This brings us closer to the heart of the matter. The term "capital" has its origins in commerce. Initially it referred to money invested or loaned, subsequently to assets such as securities, goods, and manufacturing facilities, with respect to the profit they were expected to yield.[28] What distinguishes capital is therefore not the fact that it has value but its capacity to be commercialized and to produce profit.

Capital holdings large and small

As a matter of fact, large capital holdings have a very different composition than small ones. This is why they consistently generate much higher returns, as we saw in the previous section. Small capital holdings largely consist of money held in savings or checking accounts at banks. In mid-sized estates, home ownership as a rule accounts for more than half the total value. Things change once the capital owner has passed the million-euro threshold. In capital holdings of around 5 million the share of real estate, including rental income, is about 20 percent. In estates worth over 10 million,, less than 10 percent is made up of residential real estate. The truly wealthy possess above all shares and partnerships in corporations, as well as—primarily in the Anglo-Saxon world—derivatives and other financial products.

Interestingly, access to company assets shows a similar distribution today as it did in the nineteenth century. In Germany, more than 90 percent of company assets are owned by the wealthiest 10 percent of all families, the largest share of which in turn is owned by the wealthiest 1 percent. The latter own almost 80 percent of all privately held shares, while 90 percent of the population do not own any share capital. In the Anglo-Saxon countries, share ownership is somewhat more widespread due to partially privatized old age security, but the really large portfolios are in the hands of the super-rich.

Consumption or profit

It has become common usage to subsume a life insurance or a family home under the same category of "capital" as a company with

10,000 employees. But there are significant differences between the two. A life insurance is taken out to be used up at some time point. A family home is a place to live. Capital designated to be consumed at some point does not represent capital. Capital is invested in order to make a return. Below a certain minimum threshold—generally significantly above one million—it is therefore not capital. Only above this threshold, as we have seen, can significant returns be realized.

Some upper middle-class households may own rental property or hold shares in their portfolio, but these usually represent savings not for the purpose of generating returns (which are rarely high enough for a living) but rather as a nest egg to protect against inflation, which can be cashed in in an emergency. This is the reason why about 90 percent of Germans do not touch shares. Share portfolios are profitable for those interested in the returns but extremely hazardous if one *is forced to* sell the shares at some point. Savings can quickly lose half their value or more.

Workplace vs investment

The situation is similar in the case of owners and managers of small and mid-sized enterprises who control the working capital of their firms. But this capital is simply the basis of their work, just like the home they own is the place they live. It is not an investment that was made to turn a profit. Mid-sized firms rarely distribute significant amounts of capital income.

There are additional differences between assets and capital. An individual who has invested money in an enterprise with thousands of employees has power over the lives of these people and their families, as well as the future of an entire region. If this enterprise goes bankrupt as a result of bad decisions, it will have far-reaching consequences. By contrast, if an individual owns an old palace and due to incompetence or lack of interest lets it fall into disrepair, this will be of interest only to the cultural heritage agency. Thus capital entails power, whereas assets as such do not.

Saving does not create capital

There is a third important difference: we accumulate assets primarily by savings from our working income. It would be a futile undertaking to try to accumulate *capital* in this way. The average German family has annual savings of just 1,300 euros. Based on current zero interest rates, it would take almost a thousand years to save the first million. Even individuals with higher incomes are far from earning enough to accumulate significant amounts of capital. Capital does not grow out of savings from working incomes but is a result of reinvesting the returns of already existing capital. It thus originates not in personal work but in the work of others. Joseph Schumpeter noted that you cannot attain the status of a capital owner by living frugally and saving large portions of your wage. "The bulk of accumulation comes from profits and hence presupposes profits—this is in fact the *sound* reason for distinguishing saving from accumulating."[29]

The fact that large holdings of capital do not originate in working income is also indicated by the fact that everywhere in the world capital ownership has a much more unequal distribution than working income. While the working income of the top 10 percent of earners rarely exceeds 2530 percent of all incomes, the share of the richest 10 percent in capital assets is more than twice as high.

20,000 years of drudgery

The situation is most evident at the very top. The capital assets of the 500 richest Germans add up to 625 billion euros. Even the 500 top executives with annual salaries of 20 million euros each would have to work to a ripe old age while saving all of their salaries in order to accumulate this capital. Never mind 500 average earners who would have had to start in the Stone Age 20,000 years ago, when Central Europe was largely unsettled, living on nothing but air and the wild berries of the forest.

In 2013 the ten wealthiest German families received a total of 2.4 billion euros in dividends. Even in the absence of a modest lifestyle, enough will be left over for reinvestment. In large corporations with a majority ownership in the hands of a family dynasty, a significant portion of profits is not even distributed but accumulated directly in the company.

Further evidence for the independence of capital accumulation from savings is the fact that since the 1980s stock markets in industrialized countries have had a negative financial balance. This means that through dividend payments and share buybacks, corporations distributed more money to their investors than the total they collected by issuing new shares or increasing their capital stock. Internal capital accumulation in share companies has been occurring for a long time completely independent of external financing. Instead it is based on the reinvestment of part of their profits. This is precisely the process that Schumpeter describes.

Thus savings are unrelated to capital and interest payments on savings are unrelated to capital income. The average saver does not have the privilege of living comfortably on the work of others.

3.3 Inherited privilege: Capital feudalism

The model of capitalism that emerged in the second half of the twentieth century differed from its precursors (as well as from its current form) above all in the fact that, even for children of poor parents, it was possible to rise to the middle class, and even to the upper middle class. The democratization of education, tuition-free university, workers' rights through union struggle, financial improvements for industrial workers, the expansion of public services—all contributed to the growth of the middle class, and for many the personal experience of advancement.

For the middle class it really was true at the time that whoever was talented, worked hard, and was not afflicted by particularly bad luck was able to advance and live significantly better than their parents or grandparents. Family wealth and inheritance were no longer the only route to prosperity. Good education, talent, and commitment also opened up real opportunities to the children of less privileged families for a career and prosperity.

Thin air

But even during the happy days of what in Germany was called the "Rhenish model" of capitalism, the rule applied that the higher the level of income, the thinner the air would become and the smaller the number of those making it who did not come from a "good home". Michael Hartmann, a sociologist of elites, sums it up as follows: "While the expansion of the education system made it easier for the offspring of the popular classes to acquire a doctorate, it did not open up access to the top executive level of the German economy."[30]

The old tradition has remained unchanged: origin counts more than talent, family background beats performance. The statistics have remained surprisingly stable over many decades. Of the top executives of Germany's 100 largest companies, roughly half are from the upper class. Another third have an upper middle class background, and only 15 percent emerged from the middle or working classes. The position of Chairman of the Board is almost exclusively the domain of descendants of the upper middle and upper classes, which, according to Hartmann's classification, represent the wealthiest 3.5 percent of the population.[31]

Family clans

Conditions are similar in other European countries. Hartmann believes that this is due primarily to "the obvious importance of family clans in the economy".[32] This of course applies above all to large enterprises still owned by family dynasties, which in Germany, Italy, and the Netherlands play a prominent role in the economy. In such enterprises, top positions are directly inherited. However, in corporations that are not owned by a single family, recruitment mechanisms also tend to follow the classic feudal pattern.

How this works could recently be observed in the case of Volkswagen, a corporation with strong employee representation on the board and the state of Lower Saxony as a shareholder with veto powers. When Ferdinand Piëch and his wife resigned their board positions as a result of disagreements with the former CEO Martin Winterkorn, the Volkswagen board nominated two nieces of company patriarch Piëch as new members of the board. What aside from blood ties qualified the two women to be involved in corporate strategy of the world's largest carmaker, with almost 600,000 employees and 200 billion euros in annual sales, remains a well-kept secret. Even their uncle Ferdinand seems to have had some doubts.

According to Hartmann, only in public and cooperative enterprises, or in those with the state as majority owner, can a different selection method for top positions be observed. Career prospects are twice as high for candidates from the general population. Correspondingly, the economic elite in countries where the state plays a greater role, for example in Scandinavia, is slightly less determined by family background than in Germany. To the extent that changes can be observed over recent years in Europe as a whole, the trend is towards even further closure among the upper ranks.

The brief heyday of the performance principle

According to statistics presented by Piketty, in the nineteenth and early twentieth centuries, 80 to 90 percent of all private wealth was inherited. It was not until the decades following World War II that the working middle class was in a position to accumulate personal wealth—to the point that in the 1970s, the share of the upper class in total wealth had declined to about 30 percent. This period was the first time in recent history that more than half of all wealth was not passed down from previous generations.

This heyday of the performance principle, however, lasted less than a decade. In the early 1980s, inheritances had regained their dominant position, registering further gains in subsequent years. In 2010, more than two-thirds of all wealth was inherited from previous generations. The distribution of wealth has since changed once again in favour of the richest. Only 40 percent of all wealth in industrialized countries belongs to middle-class families.

Summing up his findings, Piketty states that "[t]he very high concentration of capital is explained mainly by the importance of inherited wealth and its cumulative effects".[33] He mentions another interesting figure in this context. Guess how large is the share of the population in every generation who inherit more than the lower half of the population earns during a lifetime? In the year 1870 it was 10 percent, today it is 15 percent. This figure shows that by now, inheritance plays a major role in the upper middle class. Far beyond the reach of even high earners, however, are the hundreds of millions or even billions in capital that in the upper class are passed down from one generation to the next, as a rule without being subject to significant taxation.

Inheritance or marriage

At the top of the wealth pyramid, where we are dealing not only with wealth but with capital, the changes in the relevance of inherited wealth just described never occurred: capital is owned by those who inherit it. This has been the rule since the nineteenth century, everything else is the exception. Of course the first-generation Rockefellers and Fords, the Jobs', Gates', Bezos', and Zuckerbergs who started with little and are leaving their descendants billion-dollar empires did and do exist. Cases of such careers, however, almost never happen in established markets but only in newly emerging markets where enterprises can in fact start out with little capital and grow very rapidly. Such cases are much rarer than such fabulous stories of self-made billionaires seem to suggest.

The German business daily *Handelsblatt* recently published calculations according to which among the country's wealthiest business families, merely 10 percent are first generation. This means that 90 percent have not built up their own enterprises but took them over from their parents.[34] The surest and best way to become a capital owner continues to be the choice of the right parents.

Marriage may also make it possible to start a career as capital owner. Among the women in Germany nowadays regarded as "major business personalities", several are from modest backgrounds. Liz Mohn, ruler over Bertelsmann, started out as a dental assistant, Friede Springer as a nanny. The recently deceased Johanna Quandt, a major BMW shareholder, was originally a secretary, while Maria-Elisabeth Schaeffler, owner of the Schaeffler Group, started out as a student who failed to complete any of her university programs. All the women just mentioned today play in the billionaires' league. Of course, there are also a few men who have managed to gain access to the exclusive club of capital owners through marriage.

Capital as an exclusive good

Capital under capitalism is an *exclusive* good, that is, one to which most people will have no access. You would quickly find out if, without the benefit of marriage or inheritance or enough money of your own, you were to take the chance of setting up your own business and went to a bank with a good innovative idea to secure the necessary financing.

In fact, even most large enterprises got off the ground only because financing was available through family connections. In his book *Patriarchs*, the Swiss author Alex Capus recounts the life stories of ten Swiss enterprises that laid the groundwork for what today are global corporations: Rudolf Lindt, chocolate manufacturer; Carl

Frank Bally, shoe manufacturer; Julius Maggi, king of spices; Antoine Le Coultre, maker of precision watches; Henri Nestlé, founder of the eponymous food giant; Johann Jacob Leu, banker; Fritz Hoffmann-La Roche, who established a pharmaceutical corporation based on ineffective cough medicine; Charles Brown and Walter Boveri, founders of what is now Asea Brown Boveri; Walter Gerber, inventor of processed cheese; and Emil Bührle, weapons manufacturer and supplier to the German Wehrmacht.

No dishwashers

As different as their industries may have been, the ten individuals share one thing in common. They either came from a rich family or they married into one. The author sums up the results of his study as follows: "It is clear that the majority of the enterprises examined here would hardly have thrived after their start-up period without the money of their fathers-in-law; the other four patriarchs did not depend on their wives' money since they themselves were wealthy. It seems that in old Europe, the classic career as a dishwasher rarely led to the top of the economic hierarchy."[35]

This result is not due to the Swiss setting or the historical period in which these enterprises were established. The book *Visionaries Who Succeed*,[36] published in 2006, portrays innovative young German entrepreneurs. We meet programmers, engineers, and pharmaceutical researchers. The same picture emerges: two of the entrepreneurs featured inherited their businesses, one started out with a bank guarantee from his stepfather, one team of founders benefited from its connection with a university hospital, and one was the beneficiary of a government start-up fund. As a rule, private banks were not willing to support the young entrepreneurs, even though they all had good ideas and a business model that turned out to be successful.

The only chance to set up a firm without the backing of wealthy fathers or in-laws is to secure private or public venture capital, which is rarely available. Private financing is usually available only for firms with short-term prospects of being listed on the stock exchange or of being sold, which forces such firms to adopt particular priorities and profit goals. Public financing or loan guarantees do help some young entrepreneurs, but especially in Germany and Europe are available only to a very limited extent. Of course you can also scrape together all your savings and put up your home as collateral. Many small firms start out in this fashion. However, both with respect to industry and growth potential, such ventures tend to face strong restrictions. Exceedingly few make it to the top in this way.

Stable dynasties

In the final analysis, inheritance accounts for the trans-generational, dynastic stability of the capitalist upper class that so much resembles the old hereditary nobility. In his classic *The Reich Dissolved, the Rich Remained*, Bernt Engelmann documents such striking continuities particularly in twentieth-century Germany. Based on last names, he demonstrates "that the money and power elite of the kingdom of Bavaria that was assembled in the Chamber of the Imperial Council of 1913 was able to pass on intact all of their wealth and most of the social positions to their descendants of today—notwithstanding two lost world wars, complete monetary devaluation, abolition of the nobility's privileges, as well as attempted land and other reforms."[37]

The rejection of feudal privileges was a central element of the Enlightenment. All human beings are equal and should therefore start out with the same opportunities, with talent and performance determining the social status of the individual rather than family pedigree assigned by birth. In contrast to those who call themselves liberals today, the great pioneer of liberalism in the nineteenth century, John Stuart Mill, was committed to true liberal traditions. He was a vehement opponent of inherited privileges and demanded government intervention: "Whatever fortune a parent may have inherited, or still more, may have acquired, I cannot admit that he owes to his children, merely because they are his children, to leave them rich, without the necessity of any exertion. [...] Without supposing extreme cases, it may be affirmed that in a majority of instances the good not only of society but of the individuals would be better consulted by bequeathing to them a moderate, than a large provision."[38]

"Feudal-plutocratic" inheritance law

In the middle of the twentieth century, the liberal economist Alexander Rüstow attacked the "feudal-plutocratic" inheritance law on which capitalism had been based since its inception. "The inherited inequality of opportunity is the essential institutional structural element through which feudalism continues to exist in market society, turning it into a plutocracy, the rule of the rich."[39] One might also put it as follows: It is capitalism that accounts for the survival of feudalism in the market economy. For without the current inheritance law, there would be no capital ownership concentrated in a few hands passed on from generation to generation, and without this legal basis there would be no capitalism, which rests on private ownership of the economy.

To get to the root of the problem, Rüstow continued the liberal tradition of John Stuart Mill, calling for limiting individual inheritance to an amount that a normal earner could actually accumulate in a lifetime through work and savings. In current purchasing power, and including those with higher salaries, this would amount to about one million euros per child. Thus, while the middle class would be able to pass on its wealth, big capital would not. Establishing such an inheritance law would not just be a minor reform of capitalism, but one that would deprive it of its foundation and require institutional changes in the economic property regime.

At least at the top, capitalism has always been what Piketty refers to as a "patrimonial society"—a society in which it is primarily the size of the "paternal inheritance" that decides who will and who will not be rich.

3.4 Upward mobility was yesterday: the "new middle class" moves to the bottom

You can't blame former German chancellor Gerhard Schröder for failing to announce the reforms he would later implement. The cigar-smoking Social Democrat had already used the slogan "The New Middle" in the election campaign of 1998. Even if a slightly different meaning was intended at the time, a "new middle" was indeed the result of his seven years in office from 1998–2005. Liberalization of the labour market and cuts to social security and pensions (reforms known in Germany as "Hartz IV", after Schröder's key adviser Peter Hartz) did shift the middle of society downward, in this sense creating a *new* middle—one with lower incomes and a significantly less secure life.

The "old middle" consisted of millions of people in normal jobs: plumbers and flight attendants, lab managers and assistants, bus drivers and teachers, university staff and hospital doctors, programmers and engineers. As a rule, they all worked full-time, personal circumstances permitting, had permanent contracts, a good salary, and the prospect of a more or less secure old age. Many were organized in trade unions, with collective agreements ensuring that their incomes would rise, if not rapidly, at least gradually. Life was not a walk in the park, but relatively predictable and could be planned.

Low wages, work contracts, and temporary work

The decades following World War II were the time of the "old middle" when the goal of former economics minister and chancellor Ludwig Erhard was largely achieved: "to leave behind once and for all the old conservative social structure with a thin upper class and a large lower class by means of broad-based mass purchasing power." Yet "once and for all" was not to be the case. At some point in the 1980s or 1990s, depending on the country, the worthy goal of prosperity for all was forgotten in all European countries. It happened precisely at the time when politicians like Reagan and Thatcher and their followers went to work to make capitalism once again genuinely *capitalist*.

In many sectors of German society the "old middle" has become a thing of the past. As a result of labour market reforms, privatization, spending cuts and job cuts in the public service, it has been replaced by a "new middle". Low-wage workers, temporary and limited contract employees, the self-employed, and part-timers whose meagre incomes are not subject to any collective agreement. Many of them are forced to move from one short-term job to another, their lives characterized by insecurity and uncertainty.

The incomes of this "new middle" are roughly 20 percent below the level what was paid for comparable work in the year 2000. In some sectors, the decline is even more dramatic. While these changes had started prior to Gerhard Schröder's time in office and continued after him, the so-called Agenda 2010—his government's reform program co-written with the industrial and employer associations made up of capital income recipients—was the catalyst of this radical change.

Deutsche Post and Lufthansa pushing down wages

With these changes any explanation of income differences in society's middle in terms of the performance principle has become completely ludicrous. When in the past the doorbell rang and a delivery person dropped off a package for us, this individual was a civil servant. He had a job for life, a good income and the prospect of a decent pension. In the mid-1990s, the postal service was privatized and turned into a share company, which by the year 2000 was listed on the stock exchange. Since that time, newly-hired delivery personnel are no longer civil servants, earn significantly less, and frequently are on a limited contract.

The time came when the privatized post office was no longer content with just this form of wage dumping. In 2015 it set up a subsidiary, DHL Delivery. Its employees are not paid according to the parent company's wage rates but receive 20 percent less. Company pensions were eliminated as well. Somewhat cynically, these delivery workers on limited contracts were then offered permanent positions in the subsidiary. Of course management was unconcerned about how these employees were supposed to pay their rent and feed their families—a lack of concern also on the part of the federal government which, with the power of the shares it controlled, could have stopped the wage squeeze.

The postal service is not an isolated case. The model just described has become a template in many sectors of the economy. The formerly state-owned airline Lufthansa, completely privatized by 1997, also follows this model. In business jargon this is referred to as the *separation between brand and production*. The brand is the marketing platform that the customer associates with quality. Reserving a flight with Lufhansa feels different from buying a seat from low-cost airline Ryanair. The brand name is used as a cover for setting up different individual companies—so-called platforms—with vastly different working conditions and wage rates. Lufthansa, for example, has created the subsidiary Eurowings as its own low-cost carrier. The fact that this outfit is somehow part of Lufthansa is supposed to reassure customers, while low wages and poor working conditions make for good dividends.

Farewell to the performance principle

This "wage dumping" model reaches its state of perfection when management succeeds in having the different platforms with their varying wage rates compete with each other internally, undercutting each other in their fight for jobs. In large technology firms, departments are pitted against each other in order to produce the lowest-cost solution. Thus German engineers have to compete with engineers from Belarus, or German software developers with their

Indian counterparts. To the extent that internal competition works, management and shareholders win.

Outsourcing jobs or entire sectors through contract work or temporary employment are playing a similar role in many firms. As a result of such arrangements, work performance and income, hard work and success, no longer bear any justifiable relation with each other. Whether on the assembly lines of German auto manufacturers, the service counters of the post office, or in the cars of German trains, people work side by side who have a similar education, do the same jobs, work equally hard, yet take home vastly different wages. Obviously a postal worker today does not put in 20 or 30 percent less work than did her predecessors with a guarantee of lifetime employment just because her wage has declined by this amount.

Subsidies for the "less capable"?

The Hartz IV labour reforms mentioned above provide for "subsidies for employees of reduced work capability", a euphemism for paying public subsidies to skilled workers who lost their jobs but are re-hired on contract at half their previous wage for doing the same work. Obviously this radical wage drop that forces workers to apply for supplementary welfare payments is not due to a sudden 50 percent reduction in the skilled workers' ability. The same has happened to employees that the privatized postal office shifted to its low-wage subsidiary DHL Delivery or who have found employment with one of its competitors whose business models are all based on low wages.

Even a good education no longer guarantees a secure life. The second largest group in Germany's low wage sector today following the unskilled are academics. One reason is that public expenditure cuts have turned German universities into low-wage zones. The large majority who fail to secure one of the small number of sought-after full professorships are paying for their passion for research and teaching with a lifetime of poor living conditions and contract jobs.

Family background before talent

Even access to education is today no longer primarily a matter of individual talent. In many fields the rule is: *family background before talent*. We are familiar with this principle from international universities that call themselves elite universities, by which they seem to suggest above all the hereditary passing on of the best education opportunities and the best positions. This principle is increasingly coming to dominate other educational institutions as well.

In the United States parental income is a fairly reliable predictor of whether or not the offspring will go to university, and if so which institution it will be. For those aiming to get into Harvard, an IQ level like that of Harvard (and Yale) graduate George W. Bush will not pose an obstacle if mom and dad make generous donations, and preferably are Harvard graduates themselves. The average annual income of the parents of students attending Harvard is around 450,000 dollars—the average income of the wealthiest 2 percent of American families.

Exclusive educational institutions

Top European universities are only slightly more democratic. The average annual parental income of students at Sciences Po, one of the two French elite universities that are the gateway for most leadership positions in French politics and business, is estimated to be 90,000 euros. In contrast to Harvard, the offspring of the top 10 percent of earners may make it into those schools.

In Germany such exclusive—in the sense of excluding a large majority—educational institutions did not exist until a policy called "initiative for excellence" started to change things. Tuition rates at Germany's private universities are significantly below those at Harvard or Stanford, but they are high enough to ensure that the children of the top 10 percent dominate the cohort. Even in the much-maligned "mass universities", tuition fees and inadequate student aid are resulting in much stronger social selection than was the case in the German educational system of the 1970s and 1980s.

Much debated but still unchanged, the three-tiered German school system with its early selection process at the end of Grade 4 reinforces dependence of individual educational opportunities on family background. While this system existed in the decades after Word War II, its implications were less dramatic then than they are today simply because there was less social inequality and poor and wealthy families lived in the same neighbourhoods. As a result, the three different types of schools did not differ as much in terms of their infrastructure and level of teaching.

The Gatsby curve

It is a generally recognized fact in economics, to the extent the discipline deals with such issues, that greater social inequality significantly reduces social mobility, i. e. the opportunity for social advancement. In this context, U.S. economist Alan Krueger has coined the phrase "the Great Gatsby curve" to sum up the general results of his empirically based country studies.

Movie buffs know the story of Jay Gatsby, the main character in a novel by F. Scott Fitzgerald published in 1925. There have been several cinematic treatments of the novel, the most recent in 2013 with Leonardo DiCaprio in the lead role. Gatsby lived the American dream that millions of people are still dreaming today, making it from poor beginnings to multi-millionaire—even if the black market dealings that made his career possible may not be part of the official version of the myth. But regardless of how he succeeded, for Alan Krueger the name Gatsby signifies the career opportunities a society offers. The Gatsby curve represents the probability of such a career as dependent on the degree of social inequality. Krueger is not referring to the classic career from dishwasher to millionaire, but rather the general opportunity to achieve a higher social status than one's parents.

Krueger's findings are clear. In countries where the gap between rich and poor is particularly wide, such as Chile or Brazil, but also the United States, the road from the bottom to the top is exceptionally steep. In contrast, egalitarian societies such as Denmark or Sweden offer greater opportunities to work your way to the top. Germany occupies a middle position, though conditions since the turn of the century and the advent of the Agenda 2010 reforms have clearly changed things for the worse.

Currently, in Germany, 1.6 million children are growing up in families dependent on social welfare payments ("Hartz IV"). Few of them will ever have any real opportunities for social improvement. Being born in poverty means a life in poverty—this brutal historical fact, true for centuries, is once again the rule for most people. It was not capitalism but welfare states with their social security and well-funded public education systems that in the second half of the twentieth century created the conditions in which many were able to realize the dream of social advancement. Those times are gone.

4. ROBBER BARONS AND TYCOONS—POWER INSTEAD OF COMPETITION

4.1 Industrial oligarchs: no chances for newcomers

Goethe once remarked that "we never hear more talk about freedom than when one party wants to subdue another".[40] In much the same sense we could say that rarely is there as much talk of market and competition as in times when functioning markets and real competition are globally in retreat and further marginalized by technological developments as well as political decisions.

The *marketization* of our society, its handing over to the *market* or the *rule of the market* are frequently held responsible for negative phenomena in our time. Neoliberals who do away with government regulation and push through privatizations we call "market radicals", not realizing that we are falling for an illusion they have created to obscure the actual effects of their policies. The market represents anonymous competition between parties who in principle are equal—it symbolizes a sphere that may be cold, money-driven and commercial, but in principle largely free. This image has little to do with reality. Free markets are anything but the life-blood of capitalism. Rather, they tend to interfere with high profits and are therefore best avoided.

Adam Smith already observed the underlying mentality when in 1776 he bemoaned "the wretched spirit of monopoly" by which merchants and manufacturers were obsessed. Business people in the same trade would rarely get together "but the conversation ends in a conspiracy against the public, or in some contrivance to raise prices."[41]

Businessmen or shopkeepers?

The French economic historian Fernand Braudel, who studied the emergence of capitalism in great depth, emphasized the importance of the distinction between capitalism and the market economy. In his lectures on the "Dynamic of Capitalism" delivered at Johns Hopkins University in 1976, he states: "There are two types of exchange: one is down-to-earth, is based on competition, and is almost transparent; the other, a higher form, is sophisticated and domineering... the capitalist sphere is located in the higher form."[42]

The origin of capitalism, according to Braudel, is not equal exchange but *unequal exchange*. The germ cell of capitalist economic relations was not the small-town market square where everybody could offer their products and everybody could compare prices and demand. Rather, it was long-distance trade which on account of the long transportation routes required large sums of capital and was therefore open only to those who had capital and access to bank loans and drafts. In long distance trade, only the merchant knew both sides—supply and demand—and possessed *exclusive* information that other market participants lacked. In Braudel's view, the early capitalist was a merchant who maintained trade relations with India, China, or Arabia, was present at the large fairs in Antwerp and Lyon and later at stock exchanges and in international trade centres. It was not the shopkeeper in the centre of Madrid.

Shopkeepers have indeed rarely accumulated great riches. The wealth of trading towns and their wealthiest citizens was founded on international business relations. This is where capital was invested and multiplied, at times with fantastic profits. Only the exclusive minority who already owned capital was able to participate. As a result, the number of merchants remained limited, guaranteeing that their profits would not be squeezed by excessive competition. The need for access to the exclusive good "capital" meant that wealthy merchant families frequently emerged directly from the old seigneural landed dynasties. In late fourteenth-century Florence, as Braudel notes, the old feudal nobility and the new merchant *grande bourgeoisie* could no longer be distinguished. The old upper class thus gave birth to the new upper class.

Closed markets

In the industrial age as well, the typical capitalist market is not one of open competition among many suppliers but rather the oligopoly. An oligopoly is defined as a market where a few large firms have established themselves and new entrants have virtually no chance to join. In key industrial sectors, the stabilization of oligopolies comes about primarily for technological reasons. The more mature a product, the more sophisticated the production facilities tend to be, and the more extensive the volume of capital and know-how needed for the establishment of new firms. In addition, a typical effect of industrial mass production is what economists call economies of scale or the benefit of large size. The more products of a particular kind are produced, the lower the cost of the individual product. For this reason alone a small firm will rarely be able to challenge a large firm.

Take the example of the auto sector. Immediately after World War II, when cars were still a luxury, 80 companies tried to get a foothold in the expanding German auto manufacturing industry. Just prior to the world economic crisis 30 were left. Currently there are three large German auto manufacturers. The global market is dominated by just over a dozen producers. The production of cars nowadays requires know-how and patents worth billions, extensive automated production lines, significant research and development budgets, and a global network of suppliers and dealers. The chance of a new firm entering such a market on its own steam is nil.

A market in which the initial investment is beyond what a young entrepreneur can manage is a closed market, even in the absence of any legal barriers. However, such barriers do continue to play a role as well. Monopolies awarded by the state continue to exist in the form of patents and copyrights. Such legal rules further contribute to closing off business fields occupied by established firms against young, innovative competitors.

Increased capital requirements

In the early nineteenth century when heavy industry was in the process of being established, it was possible to set up a business even in this sector with relatively limited resources. The start-up capital in Germany's coal and steel sector in the 1850s was around 2–3 million marks. Entry to the expanding textile industry was possible at an even lower price. Average citizens of course did not have this amount of capital, but the upper class certainly did. That's why many new firms were set up. But things would soon change. In the course of industrialization, capital requirements increased, and the average capital of the 100 largest German enterprises between 1887 and 1927 grew from 9.4 to 59 million Marks.

Certain industries would soon require much more. In the steel industry, which prospered with the construction of railways, investment costs rose significantly with the introduction of the Bessemer process. Subsequently, only very large enterprises were able to survive. No new firms were established, other than those resulting from the fusion of existing firms. Instead, huge conglomerates emerged that squeezed out any competitors that were not able to grow at the same speed. In 1901 U.S. Steel, one of the largest steel companies in the world at the time, had 1.4 billion dollars in capital.

Giants of the service industry

In most of the important service industries, a similar cycle occurred as in other industries, from competition to oligopoly, from open to closed markets. Global retail today is dominated by giant U.S. and European chains such as Metro, Wal-Mart or Carrefour with production on different continents. Much like the old merchants, by controlling the access routes to consumers they can transform their market power and their exclusive position vis-a-vis producers into high profits.

Upon closer inspection even some so-called manufacturing enterprises turn out to be nothing by trading chains. The U.S. sportswear producer Nike, for instance, achieved its success in large part as a result of deciding not to do any of its own manufacturing, working instead with low-price contract suppliers in a range of different countries. Instead of committing capital to machines and labour, Nike opted for investing in strategic alliances with retailers in the United States, managing to gain control of about 80 percent of the U.S. market for certain types of running shoes. Thanks to this market power Nike can now dictate to retailers what shoes from other suppliers they may and may not put on their shelves.

Another example for the establishment of market domination after a brief period of lively competition in the service industries is mobile communications. When, in the late 1990s, the technology had its breakthrough, initially there was a large number of new companies starting up. Competition was intense, prices dropped. By now this phase is over. In Germany, a *de facto* duopoly has survived: T-Mobile, which is part of Telekom, and Vodafone. The third provider, a cooperation between E-Plus and O2, is falling further and further behind. In other countries, the situation is similar. Once again this is a result of increased capital requirements. Thus smartphones require much stronger networks than the old cell phones that were used exclusively for talk. The implication is that providers have to invest billions in network expansion. This is the kind of capital you have to have, and the investment makes sense only if you have a very large customer base. New start-ups in this industry are therefore a thing of the past.

Hegemony and dependency

As early as 1959, the German weekly *Die Zeit* described the business landscape in the United States in the following terms: "In fact only

150 of the total of 4.2 million companies in industry, commerce, and trade account for about half of the country's overall production capacity. In many industries the market share of the four or five largest firms amounts to 60 percent or more."[43]

By now such distributions of market share apply globally. Thus three multinational mining companies control half of world trade in iron ore. Almost the entire trade in derivatives on world financial markets is concentrated in a few large investment banks. One of the largest corporations, Glencore, controls the lion's share of raw material trade in zinc, lead, and copper. The digital industry has been monopolized by a small number of companies from Silicon Valley.

In Germany the so-called *Mittelstand* (referring to smaller and mid-sized firms) is frequently described as the backbone of the economy. Compared to other national economies, Germany does indeed still have a relatively broad sector of mid-sized firms, many of which are international market leaders in their specialized fields. However, the picture changes somewhat in light of the fact that the 100 largest German enterprises account for greater sales than the hundreds of thousands of small and mid-sized firms combined.

In the German food retail industry, for instance, the four largest chains account for about 85 percent of total sales. If one of these giants decides to remove the products of one of its suppliers from its shelves, it means almost certain ruin for that supplier. It is thus evident how negotiating power is distributed. Market domination in food retail tends to be exerted to push prices down. By contrast, in the retail market for gasoline, 70 percent of which is in the hands of the five largest oil companies, led by BP and Shell, consumers end up paying higher prices.

In any event, in Germany as elsewhere—whether in steel or chemicals, automobile manufacturing, pharmaceuticals or electrical engineering, telephony or transport—it is a small number of large corporations controlling the most important markets. On account of their size and influence, moreover, they can rely on the helping hand of the state in times of risk or crisis.

Fictitious diversity: the modular system

The model of an economy dominated by a few corporations that can secure the largest share of the pie for themselves was established as early as the end of the nineteenth century. What has changed over past decades is the degree of integration between large corporations on a global scale by way of takeovers and cooperative arrangements, as well as the increasingly strong homogenization of their products as a result of using the same suppliers.

More than 10 years ago, for example, the so-called modular system was introduced in the automobile industry. Ever since, different model cars from different manufacturers are built "on the same platform", i.e. based on the same modules of suppliers. This system is responsible for the frequent instances and high costs of recalls. One manufacturer's recall forces the entire sector to check whether their own vehicles contain similar modules.[44]

Ford fights for its competitors

The existence of such a system was indirectly confirmed by the memorable appearance in late 2008 of the CEO of U.S. car producer Ford, Allan Mulally, in the U.S. Congress. Mulally begged Representatives to commit government support to failing competitors Chrysler and GM—successfully, as it turned out. Mulally was not motivated by a sudden bout of sympathy for the thousands of affected workers in the manufacturing plants of his competitors, let alone a principled understanding of the importance of competition. Rather, he was worried about the future of Ford, which he saw would be at stake in case of the two other car manufacturers going down since, as he was glad to explain, "the firms in the auto industry were dependent on each other in a unique fashion. The reason for this co-dependence was that the car companies were purchasing more than 90 percent from common suppliers. If one of the other domestic companies were to file for bankruptcy, the effect on Ford's own production would be felt within days if not hours. Without the parts for our just-in-time supply system, Ford would no longer be able to build cars."[45] On closer inspection the apparent diversity of producers in many markets turns out to be an illusion.

Common ownership

Aside from having the same suppliers, many presumed competitors are interconnected through lines of ownership—such as Volkswagen, Audi, Porsche, MAN, Scania, Seat, and Skoda, all of which are more or less owned by the families Porsche and Piëch. In 2011, three Swiss researchers analyzed the degree of competitiveness in the global economy. The result of their study entitled *The network of global corporate control*[46] should be a wake up call for anyone who still believes that we are living in a market economy.

The three Swiss researchers used a data bank with 37 million listed investors and companies from 2007. In the first step they identified 43,000 firms active internationally. Next they investigated to what extent these enterprises were autonomous or were controlled by others via shares or cooperative arrangements. The result was that 1,318 corporations were interlinked with at least two and on average 20 other firms. Within this group they finally identified an exclusive club of 147 corporate giants that controlled 40 percent of all 43,000 transnational enterprises.

Organized economy

One third of global trade occurs within individual corporations, a further third between the large multinationals. Taking into account their close interconnections, this means that in international economic relations markets are playing a minor role. Or, as the journalist Ulrike Herrmann puts it, the truth for the world as a whole is that "we are operating an organized economy in which the bulk of economic activities is coordinated within the borders of firms instead of through market relations between them."[47]

Yet at the same time it is true that there still are large areas of the economy where open markets exist and where a large number of small and mid-sized firms are involved in serious competition. Whether in the artisanal sector, the production of individual parts in the manufacturing sector, or in certain online services, advertising agencies, legal offices, cleaning services or cafes—in these and many other industries there is not only lively competition but also an opportunity for new entrants and others who disappear from the market. Thus there is everything that defines a functioning market.

Similarly, when new markets emerge because a product or type of product did not previously exist, there is usually intense competition with a large number of firms of which ultimately only a few survive. In mature markets, on the other hand, new firms are established only in certain niches or in corporate services, but no longer in the core business.

State support for new competition

What seems to contradict this conclusion is that in heavy industry and high technology on a global scale, new producers have entered the stage to compete with European and U.S. corporations. The contradiction dissolves if we look more closely at the conditions under which they came into existence: as a result of state intervention rather than private initiative.

It is no accident that the new players almost exclusively hail from countries that were not caught up in the market euphoria, free trade, and other aspects of the Washington Consensus. Instead, these countries initially nurtured their nascent industries in a protected domestic market with high subsidies and state-controlled capital investment. This applies to Japan, China, South Korea as well as, if to a lesser extent, the other Southeast Asian tigers. Theoretically, it is possible to enter mature markets, but only on condition that there is the support of an entire state with protection from competition for the early stages of development.

However, aside from such special cases, the rule is: in crucial markets, an oligopoly of a few large producers has become established, a structure that subsequently no longer changes. New entrants do not stand a chance in such markets. The only movement that exists is due to takeovers and mergers. It is of course possible that established enterprises disappear from the market as a result of grave management errors, but this is a rare occurrence. The image drawn by mainstream economics has little in common with this reality.

4.2 Controlled markets: market power kills innovation and quality

Firms offering their products on an oligopoly market have basically two options. They can engage in an aggressive competitive struggle with the goal of destroying the other market players. This may pay off if there is a realistic chance that in the end only one player will remain who as sole supplier will have greater profit opportunities. Or they can mark out their territories and live peacefully side by side. While there are historical examples for both approaches, the peaceful option is followed much more frequently.

Absence of ideas and inertia

And there are consequences. For without real pressure from competitors and without customers who have a choice, it makes more sense to run existing production facilities to their physical exhaustion, driving up profit through higher prices or cost cutting at the expense of service and quality. Even when established firms fail to generate new ideas and become sluggish, there is little chance of revitalizing the market under such conditions.

If German corporate giant Siemens with its philosophy of dismissing solid engineering work as "over-engineering" was in intense competition with other quality producers, there would be no reason for concern—the corporation would simply disappear. If by contrast a handful of large corporations following the same production standards determine supply, capitalism can quickly come to choke innovation and quality. Many phenomena described in the chapter on the economy's sluggish innovation capacity ultimately are the result of the concentration of market power in the hands of a small number of producers.

Many large enterprises in a variety of industries colluded in the last three decades of the nineteenth century—initially even enjoying legal status by claiming freedom of contract. In Germany between 1879 and 1886, approximately 90 cartels came into being, most of them price cartels. While nowadays cartels are illegal, collusion has to be proved before there can be regulatory action. The cost for the European economy created by collusion, according to the European Commission, amounts to 260 billion euros annually. Notwithstanding the great damage thus caused, penalty payments tend to be bearable for those who are caught.

Standard Oil and Microsoft: ambush instead of performance

If a small number of firms dominate an important market, explicit collusion is often not even necessary. Competition can simply be shut down through the use of economic power. This works particularly well for those who control a crucial raw material, a key technology, or important infrastructure.

Already prior to the American Civil War, potent finance capitalists in the U.S. had started to exploit the natural monopoly of the railways in order to take over industries that were existentially dependent on rail transport, subsequently proceeding to erect monopolies in these industries as well. This is the way the grain trade in the Midwest was brought under their control. John D. Rockefeller, founder of the legendary Standard Oil Company, made the giant oil producer even stronger by forcing the railway companies dependent on its supply to give discounts to his own company, and refuse to carry the products of his competitors.

A more recent example for exploiting a strategic position to eliminate potential competitors was Microsoft's browser war against Netscape at the beginning of the century, which in spite of the lower quality of its Internet Explorer it was able to win. It was a simple trick: Microsoft used its already existing monopoly in PC operating systems. The company spread doubts about Windows compatibility with the Netscape browser, programming error messages that would pop up randomly as soon as this browser was installed on a computer with Windows. When new versions of Windows were developed, Microsoft refused to provide to other producers the information necessary to ensure compatibility. At the same time, it offered its own Internet Explorer free of charge as an integral component of its operating system. Under those conditions, Netscape did not stand a chance, just like other producers of operating systems on the PC market did not stand a chance against Microsoft, regardless of how defective and error-prone its programs were.

Low quality prevails

There are many other examples for the use of market power to make lower-quality technologies succeed. Some of them are listed and warmly recommended for imitation in Carl Shapiro and Hal R. Varian's *Information Rules: A Strategic Guide to the Network Economy*, a management bible for internet entrepreneurs published in 1999. Concerning methods for establishing DVD standards, they write: "For example, a key source of leverage for Sony and Philips in their negotiations with others in the DVD alliance was their control over the original CD technology. Even if Sony and Philips did not develop or control the best technology for DVD, they were in the driver's seat to the extent that their patents prevented others from offering backward-compatible DVD machines."[48]

According to Shapiro and Varian, intentional lowering of quality in your own products can be a recipe for success. Thus IBM offered several de facto identical printers, with the cheapest printing more slowly as result of a chip designed specifically for this purpose. "Why did IBM deliberately degrade the performance of its printer? Company managers realized that if they made the performance of the Series E too good, it would cut into the sales of their standard model. By versioning their product, they were able to sell to the home-office market at an attractive price without cannibalizing the sales of their professional model."[49]

Software programs with lower performance, the two authors explain, were often more expensive to produce since the performance of the original high-quality product had to be lowered installing additional components. In this way the seller insures that the premium version will continue to command a higher price while at the same time profiting from those purchasing low-price products only.[50] Practices of this kind of course don't work on open competitive markets where they would be thwarted by other sellers. On today's markets, on the other hand, they represent highly effective profit-generating mechanisms for large corporations.

Cut-throat competition

The classical liberal economist Alexander Rüstow was at pains to distinguish between "performance-based competition" on the one hand and "obstruction-based" or "cut-throat competition" on the other. It is self-evident to which category the examples just discussed belong.

The legendary profits and billion-dollar estates emerging in this way are ultimately the result of eliminating competition. In the nineteenth century, industrial magnates such as Carnegie or Rockefeller, who established their dominion over newly arising markets in the industrial age by brutal means and questionable methods, were called *robber barons*. The term is quite fitting. Much like feudal lords in earlier times, the owners of such empires are able to make the entire economy pay tribute to them.

This is precisely why, in Rüstow's view, it is the explicit task of the state to establish rules and regulations for functioning markets, i.e. for markets in which competitors can gain advantages only by superior performance. Classical liberals were very clear that a weak state and a deregulated economy could never strengthen *the market*, but only the *power* of large firms over the market and thus ultimately over society as a whole. Today's neoliberals have forgotten this, are in denial, or simply lying.

The Sherman Act: Anti-trust law with bite

In 1890, the first serious anti-trust law was passed in the United States—the Sherman Antitrust Act. In contrast to later anti-trust legislation in Europe, the Sherman Act had bite. Not only demonstrable misuse of market power, but simply "the attempt to monopolize any part of the trade or commerce", according to the famous Sec. 2 of the Sherman Act, could be punished with the break-up of an enterprise. If this paragraph were still taken seriously today, the corporate empires of Google, Microsoft, Apple, and Facebook or the large U.S. investment banks could have never come into being in their present form.

In fact, there were only a few private firms to which the Sherman Act was applied in practice. Among them was the Rockefeller oil empire, Standard Oil, which, following a judgment by the U.S. Supreme Court in 1911, was broken up into 34 legally independent firms.

Nowadays, the common practice in the United States and in Europe is to consider market power as a problem only in case of demonstrated misuse, and then only if market power is the result of mergers or takeovers, not if market power is based on the occupation of future markets by individual firms, as is the rule in the digital world. Economist Walter Eucken's warning was dismissed. "Economic policy should not primarily target abuses on the part of existing powerful entities, but rather the *emergence* of powerful entities in principle, since otherwise it will have no chance of success."[51]

4.3 Data monsters: monopoly on the Internet

We have discussed that many service industries passed through a cycle similar to the large manufacturing industries—from competition to oligopoly, from open market to closed market. By now, however, there are quite a few industries in services where, rather than an oligopoly of a small number of firms, one private monopoly enterprise dominates the market. This is true in particular of most network-reliant services if they are privately owned, and of those services where so-called network effects occur.

Monopolies for court favourites

The role played by politics in the emergence of private monopolies in recent years has been rather embarrassing. Not only has politics failed to stop them, but in many sectors has actively prepared the ground for them. With the slogan "more competition", profit-oriented enterprises were entrusted with public authority, promising secure returns since they could not be exposed to competition. Such services range from energy and water supply and private highways to local and long-distance passenger transport, from city cleaning and hospitals to many other once public services.

Even more insidious than full privatization, public-private ventures have been set up as a framework for construction and infrastructure projects, as well as for a number of other public tasks. British sociologist Colin Crouch, who is internationally known for his "postdemocracy" thesis, compares public-private projects with the monopolies that were once distributed to court favourites, and which Adam Smith criticized. Where the state guarantees a minimum return and assumes the risk, while private investors make secure profits, we certainly shouldn't be speaking about a market economy.

Expensive infrastructure

There are several reasons why privatization in many sectors simply leads to the establishment of monopolies run by private profiteers. Network-based services simply do not work well with competition. Network-dependent services are defined as services that can be offered only with a initial investment in a complex and costly infrastructure. These might be railway networks for transporting passengers and goods, cable and cell phone towers for communication services, or electric lines supplying the population with energy. In contrast to the industrial sector, network-based services are tied to technological conditions that have the effect of fostering the emergence of monopolies rather than oliogopolies.

The most important reason is that the provision of such an infrastructure initially requires large investments, but subsequently can be used to supply growing numbers of customers without generating significant additional costs—at least in comparison with the initial investment. A well-constructed telephone network can be used by 5 million people or 50 million, a railway network may be used by full or empty trains. There is usually an upper limit after which new investments become necessary. However, below this threshold every additional customer generates additional income without significant extra costs.

Prices at marginal cost level

In economics, *marginal costs* refer to the costs of supplying any additional product or any additional customer, while the initial investment necessary to offer the product to the first customer are the *fixed costs*. It is obvious that services with very high fixed costs and low or irrelevant marginal costs can be offered most efficiently by an individual supplier. If all customers are supplied by one enterprise, the high fixed costs have to be invested only once, making for the lowest costs per customer. The question in what framework such goods are provided to customers, however, remains open. Economists have been preoccupied with this question since the 1930s.

The U.S. economist and statistician Harold Hotelling developed the thesis that the best approach was to use general tax revenue to cover the "fixed costs for electricity and water works, railways, and other industries with significant fixed costs in order to reduce the prices of goods and services in those industries to the level of marginal costs."[52] Under those conditions it would be possible to offer them at the lowest rates. If such services were left in the hands of private enterprises, the monopoly supplier would have the same low costs, but nothing could prevent him from making a killing. (The idea of counteracting this problem by setting up public regulatory agencies can by now be considered a failure.)

Based on this realization, in Europe, network-based infrastructure such as railways or the emerging telegraph and long distance telephone providers were largely government-built or at some time point taken over by the state. In this way, a monopoly position for private enterprises freely cashing in or dominating large sectors was to be made impossible. In the meantime, however, these realizations seem to have been forgotten—with fatal consequences.

Information: copy almost for free

However, not only network-based services have a tendency towards monopoly. The basic structure—high costs for the initial provision of a good, virtually no costs for its reproduction—is also a characteristic of the key industry that is penetrating all others and partly dominating them: the digital economy. The good traded in the digital economy is digital information, and digital information has precisely those characteristics we have just described. There may be costs involved in obtaining data or programming software for special applications, but their reproduction has almost no costs.

Now the costs for programming a word processing program or an operating system are not even close to the costs a cell phone provider has to shoulder in order to set up a network, not to mention the provision of a railway network or a comprehensive electricity grid. What then is it that keeps start-ups from stirring up established markets in the digital economy?

The network effect

There is in fact another factor that forms a much more effective barrier to entry for new market actors than high capital requirements, one that massively accelerates the trend towards monopolization: the so-called network effect. It means that certain goods or services become the more attractive the more people are already using them.

Thus the situation is precisely the opposite of what is the case in most industries. If too many people want to buy a particular model of running shoe, the price will rise and demand will decline. Overpopulated beaches tend to be a reason not to return to a particular holiday resort. Similarly, an overcrowded department store is not a draw for a shopping spree. On the other hand, the more suppliers offer their products on a particular online portal, the more attractive it will be for us make our purchases through this portal. And the more visitors a portal has, the fewer sellers can afford not to be present, even if the portal imposes very unfavourable conditions on them. A dynamic that is self-reinforcing until in the end a monopoly has emerged.

Global corporation overnight

Digital enterprises can grow extremely fast since new customers generate almost no additional costs. Compared to the rest of the economy, this is another decisive difference. A company that hits the market with a top-notch bicycle helmet—safe, light, with airbag and other extras—and is completely overwhelmed by the demand—will not be able to supply the entire European market overnight, let alone North America. The expansion of production capacity will cost time and lots of money that has to be raised. Supplier relations need to be set up and markets have to be opened up. In the digital world, on the other hand, the initial investment may be high, but reproduction will be almost cost-free, and thanks to the Internet sales over the entire globe can be had at the click of a mouse. An enterprise can thus in fact supply a market of billions overnight. Once it has become established in a particular field, the network effect will make it difficult to displace.

Self-propelling: Windows' march to victory

The same software can be downloaded an infinite number of times without any loss of quality. If the software also has the specific property of becoming increasingly useful the more people are using it, then the only challenge is reaching a critical size on the market—due to quality, tricks, and/or strong partners. From that point on, growth will be self-propelling, while competitors will be increasingly left behind. From the start, PCs were not only the better typewriters, but also tools for digital communication. For anyone wanting to exchange text or pictures with others needed software compatible with the software of as many others users as possible.

Based on Microsoft's cooperation with IBM, Windows came pre-installed on many computers, and the rest happened automatically. By the year 2000, Microsoft had a global share of over 90 percent in PC operating systems. And whoever controls the operating system has first dibs on applications from word processing to media player. The fact that a corporation thus reached sales of almost 100 billion dollars and a rate of return between 25 and 33 percent is perhaps not surprising.

Digital giants

With the development of a new class of devices, i.e. tablets and smartphones, the competitive race is on again. Microsoft's PC monopoly was of little use, and ultimately the company was unable to secure a significant share of the market. Instead, a duopoly of Apple's iOS and Google's Android was established, and only the question remains whether one side will succeed in totally eliminating the other. Programs that are not compatible with at least one of the two systems—that is to say, that do not submit to their conditions and do not pass on a share of their sales—have no perspective in the market for smartphone applications today.

The same dynamic has made Facebook into a giant. If you want to communicate with others via a social network, you will opt for one that many of your friends belong to. The same is true for Apple. The more iPhones and iPads with Apple's operating system are in use, the more firms will pay Steve Jobs's former corporation to be able to offer an app for their own services. The same applies to Android. Amazon reached the critical market threshold through its online book distribution, so far with no limits to its growth. Google's algorithm exploits the fact that its search engine is used by billions of people, processing increasing amounts of data; the storing and analysis of the data drives up its advertising revenue. As much as 10 percent of global advertising spending ends up in Google's coffers; its search engine has a global market share of 90 percent.

Freedom from competition

Someone who might figure out a smarter or even more objective search algorithm could compete with Google only if billions of users were to switch over in a short period of time. Even the Internet giants Microsoft and Facebook together have not been able to achieve this. Conversely, with GooglePlus, the company itself has failed to become a serious competitor to Facebook with its 70 percent share in social networks. Under these conditions, the belief that some smart kid might be able to break up such monopolies, which even their monopolistic competitors failed to do, can safely be consigned to the realm of fancy.

Google enjoys protection from annoying competitors not only in the area of search engines. When start-ups in Silicon Valley present their ideas to prospective investors, a typical question is: Is Google already active in this field? If it is, investors decline. Google is crowding out any competition. If an enterprise develops a new application that Google does not have in its repertoire, it will eventually be bought up. The much-celebrated venture capital market in Silicon Valley works like this: set up a firm with successful business ideas in the digital industry that you can sell to one of the large empires in five to ten years. Thus the big actors become even bigger.

Competitive freedom in the digital world therefore means freedom from competition. This is not the result of conniving executives, but is due to the basic structure of information goods. The market is a mechanism that leads to an efficient allocation of goods if there are many buyers competing for scarce resources and many suppliers providing products. Digital information, the resource of the digital world, is not scarce by nature but once in existence can be reproduced at will. There can therefore be a market for digital information only if scarcity is artificially created.

The data monsters

This does create problems as well as restricting the circle of users. The digital enterprises realized very quickly that it is much more profitable to provide software or access to its online services free of charge. The Google search engine or Gmail, just like registration on Facebook, do not cost the user anything. In the case of Apple we pay for the hardware—the iPhones and iPads—while software is included. The business model of these corporations is to establish a data monopoly by way of providing their services. Trillions of datasets about our preferences, interests, and buying habits, about our friends, our fitness or our mobility, are stored on the company's own servers in order to be analyzed by algorithms for a variety of purposes.

This information, which is at the exclusive disposal of the data monopolist, is the actual basis for doing profitable business. When the young Viennese lawyer and data protection activist Max Schrem sued Facebook for violating European privacy law in 2011, he successfully forced the corporation to hand over its file with his data. It was a PDF file that was 1,222 pages long.

Orwell on the Internet

One way of exploiting these data is to sell customized advertising space. This may appear relatively harmless. If you buy a jumper you will subsequently be flooded with ads for baby food and toys. If you buy workout equipment for a friend, you will be hearing from sellers of fitness products and perhaps energy drinks and health supplements. This may be annoying but it is not a tragedy.

However, much more is at stake. Where the happy consumer world ends and Orwell starts, profiles are constructed—profiles of specific market structures (buyers who purchase A are very likely to be interested in B three months later), profiles of customer groups, or even individual profiles. Powerful algorithms make it possible to create increasingly detailed profiles on the basis of analyzing the infinite bits of data on us that are being stored—the traces we leave with every Internet search, the data that our smartphones, tablets, or fitness watches constantly send to the servers of providers, the content in our clouds, our email correspondence, our Facebook posts, and our online purchases.

Surveillance would be perfect if the different data monsters were to cooperate and pool their data. For this reason each one of them is constantly extending its tentacles into new fields. Thus Google is interested in thermostats and our household electronics, while Google and Apple are fighting over dominance in our cars.

Uber's statistics on extramarital affairs

Basic versions of such profiles are used on the Internet today in order to sell the same thing to different buyers at different prices. This is particularly unfortunate if some algorithm has identified you as an above-average earner. Then you will be paying more for the same flight ticket or the same hotel booking than, say, your neighbour who browses the web with an old computer and has so far not been pegged as someone with extravagant tastes.

Things become really fascinating with personal profiles in which insurance companies, credit agencies, potential and actual employers, and of course secret services have a great deal of interest. When a little while ago the online taxi service Uber surprised the public with statistics on the frequency of extramarital affairs in certain areas of large U.S. cities, people were generally not amused. And when you are refused a loan because some algorithm has drawn the wrong conclusions from your circle of Facebook friends, things become very serious.

Trade monopolies and dependent producers

Data monsters do more than just store any information on our lives they get. They have increasing power over the actual producers of goods and services. Platforms like Amazon or the Apple Store have the great advantage that only they own the data on both sides of the market. Only they know all the parameters of sellers and all the contact, consumption, and payment data of customers. Buyers and sellers, on the other hand, no longer have any contact with each other.

The larger the share of trade that is shifting to the Internet and the greater the significance of retail platforms, the more ruthlessly they can exploit this power and divert a growing portion of value added to themselves. Earlier we mentioned the concentration in the German food retail trade and the dependence of their suppliers on them. But in the analogue world there are at least still a few different chains in existence. In the Internet there is a rapid development towards the monopoly of Amazon, which in the future will allow only specialized sellers to survive. This will place sellers completely at the mercy of the monopolist.

The consequences of this kind of concentration of power can be observed in the case of Apple. Apple decides what is offered on iTunes and in the Apple Store. Apple ties everything to its own software. Apple determines what is placed where in its store. And only Apple knows who the buyers are. This leads to an extreme degree of dependence of the producer on the seller. For the latter this is extremely profitable. For its placement Apple charges 30 percent of the sale price as commission, even though in contrast to a normal department store the corporation pays neither rent or heat nor wages for a sales staff.

The Internet of things: networked surplus generation

The infrastructure of the *Internet of things* occupies much the same crucial position as retail platforms with a trend towards monopolization. It is predictable that digital networks transcending the borders of firms will control the flow of material and supplies in the future. Producers no longer work for an anonymous market, but instead time and scale of demand will be determined before production begins. To some extent this is already the case today in the furniture industry. First comes the order, then production, with the benefit for the customer of receiving tailor-made products.

The largest European seller of steel, Klöckner, has recently set up a digital trading platform in order to establish the demand for steel pipes before producers start manufacturing. In this way Klöckner wants to avoid the expensive storage of pipes. This will reduce Klöckner's exposure to risk. On the whole, digitalization can increase the efficiency of production by reducing excess production that ultimately will not find a buyer.

No end to growth in storage capacity

The continuing growth in digital storage capacity will make it possible to equip all products with sensors for continuous monitoring of availability and processing of all materials, inputs, and finished products. The final link in this chain will be digitally networked refrigerators, milk cartons, coffee machines, car tires, or even toothbrushes that will automatically indicate when they are about to expire and place renewal orders.

A steel trading platform of the future could access such a network of sensors at any time. Every brick at every construction site would be connected with it, while an algorithm could calculate ahead of time when the steel girders for the second floor will be needed. The order would be passed on to the trading platform, which would bundle all orders from a region, and then invite the steel plants to an auction. Thus steel would be ordered and sold before being produced, and every ton of steel manufactured by a firm would have a known destination.[53]

Dumping pressures

Markets would continue to play a role only at the intersections where the orders for the production of individual construction elements will occur. At those points, competition would increase significantly, since practically all firms in an industry could submit bids, whereas today supplier relations play an important role. If in the end only an algorithm decides who gets the order, there will be only one criterion: the lowest price. Dependence on a digital platform and increased competitive pressure would undoubtedly imply that producers earn significantly less than they do today.

Dumping competition with declining wages and bankruptcies would be a likely outcome. The number of competitors would be further reduced and there is likely to be more inter-firm cooperation. Markets thus would play an even smaller role in the value-added chain than they already do.

Revival of the planned economy?

Does this imply that the old planned economy, which in the 1990s was generally considered a failure, is getting ready for a comeback in a modernized high-tech variant? Certainly not. In spite of the current euphoria about the potential of the "Internet of things", we should remember that the model ultimately works only for standardized products offered by many manufacturers at the same level of quality. When dealing with high technology and complicated building parts, it is unlikely that a firm will entrust its choice of suppliers to a digital platform and its algorithm.

Much the same is true for consumers. It is quite conceivable that the self-replacing milk container or vacuum bag will be successful. But who wants to have their broken refrigerator automatically replaced by the same manufacturer? Or to leave it to an algorithm to automatically order the currently cheapest model?

Notwithstanding these reservations, digital networking in the creation of value will play an increasingly important role. A central question is therefore who controls those networks and whether they may end up in the wrong hands. Since all data on production and consumption will ultimately have to come together in one or a very small number of standardized platforms, there will be extreme network effects. Currently the data monsters Google and Apple find themselves in the most promising position to become the platforms for the "Internet of things". They already control most access routes to consumers.

Data monopoly and global dominance

However, if we leave this network to profit-oriented data monopolists, there will be dramatic consequences for us all. To have control over the central infrastructure for industrial production in the twenty-first century is as if one private corporation in the twentieth century had been given authority over the total global network of railways and roads, air and water, as well as telecommunications. It would mean not only the power of imposing a fee on anyone wanting to move things by land, air, or sea, but also independently to decide who will and who will not be allowed to use roads and railways, travel the seas, and transport goods by air.

Such a corporation would be able to redirect the surplus creation of the world economy into its own coffers to such an extent that the "robber barons" of the nineteenth and twentieth centuries would appear harmless by comparison. Powerful monopolists ripping off everyone without producing anything would have finally superseded performance-driven competition between producers, with all the negative consequences this would have for the quality of products and the prosperity of the rest of us.

There is still time to change direction. But we have to do it soon, and we shouldn't assume that the market will do it for us. "Information capitalism is as incapable of regulating itself as financial market capitalism"[54], writes big-data entrepreneur and expert for artificial intelligence, Yvonne Hofstetter. The internet giants are in fact as influential as the large financial firms and the global players of industry. They all have ways and means to buy the policies they need.

The type of state emerging from an economy in which crucial markets are dominated by a few large private enterprises or even by powerful private monopolists is not a democracy but an oligarchy. Former U.S. President Jimmy Carter recently referred to the United States as an "oligarchy with limitless political corruption." He knows of what he speaks. The discrepancy between democratic claims and corporation-dominated politics is no less great in Europe, especially at the level of EU institutions. Whoever wants a democratic society must wrest power from the "robber barons" who have turned the contemporary state into their subject. In the second part of the book, we will discuss how that might be done.

4.4 The visible hand of the state

Milton Friedman, head of the Chicago School and one the most important theorists of neoliberalism, describes capitalism the way many still see it today—"a model of society organized by means of free exchange."[55] The fact that capitalism generates wealth, he maintains, is solely "an effect of the initiative and entrepreneurial spirit of individuals." State intervention set up only obstacles to development. Milton Friedman is an early example of reality loss that afflicts many economists to this day.

In contrast to the popular distinction between market and state, capitalism from the start has employed state power. Without active state intervention, capitalism would never have come into being, and without strong state support it could not have grown. "Capitalism only triumphs when it becomes identified with the state, when it is the state."[56], writes French economic historian Fernand Braudel. He points out that the merchants of early capitalism were "friends of the prince and helpers or exploiters of the state"[57], which formed the basis for their dominance over other, less privileged market actors.

To this day, nothing has changed with respect to this close connection between large enterprises and state power. As a matter of fact, the difference between rich countries and poor countries consists much less in one group having the more innovative entrepreneurs or industrious workers. Rather, the difference between the two results from one group having functioning states that can provide what a capitalist economy needs for growth and large profits, whereas the other group has weak states that do not have that capacity. This concerns, on the one hand, government services on the national level—from education and research to infrastructure and legal security. Equally important, however, is the role of the state on the international level. Above all, this concerns the state's ability to fight for raw materials and markets using money, diplomacy, and if necessary military means.

War, trade, and piracy

The military already played a decisive role in the early capitalist era. "War, trade, piracy / A trinity that none may sever"[58], as Goethe's Faust learns as an entrepreneur who, with Mephistopheles's help, is building a global enterprise based on these principles. As a matter of fact, capitalism has been global since its inception. Seen in this light, globalization is nothing new. Capitalism and international trade have always belonged together, and thus the control of global trade routes has always been very important, which in turn was a question of military strength.

When the centre of power for global trade shifted from the Mediterranean to Northern Europe, this had little to do with the market and competition but a great deal with brute force. Since about 1570, the Mediterranean world was constantly attacked, battered and pillaged by northern European ships and merchants. The world's first stock company was the Dutch United East India Company, established in 1602. In this as well as in other trading companies set up for the purpose of colonial trade, the transition from capitalist business to waging war was fluent. There apparently were years when the United East India Company extracted most of its revenue not from the trade in goods but from seizing competing ships. That the northern Europeans eventually triumphed over the once thriving cities of the Mediterranean was primarily due to the fact that thanks to a superior fleet, with their soldiers and canons they managed to take over the most important trade routes.

War capitalism

The miraculous profits generated by these trading companies, however, depended on state support in a number of other respects. A guaranteed monopoly over long-distance trade and military units for conducting raids in the colonies were particularly useful. In his book *King Cotton*,[59] Sven Beckert calls this early form of capitalism *"war capitalism"*.

War capitalism was characterized by violence rather than competition, the ruthless expropriation of land and labour rather than property rights, and slavery rather than wage labour. And for all this the early capitalists needed the state and the military.

The economic historian Karl Polanyi sarcastically describes the economic role of military force in those early days of the capitalist era. "[I]f the region in question happened to be rich in raw materials required for European manufactures, while no pre-established harmony ensured the emergence of a craving after European manufactures on the part of the natives"[60], then trade followed the war fleet which had to prepare the ground. It is not fundamentally different today. Capitalism carries within itself a certain degree of war capitalism, while the ruthlessness with which this aggressive side of the profit interest manifests itself depends on the international distribution of power.

According to a widely held assumption, the Industrial Revolution in England had its origins primarily in free enterprise and free markets. On the contrary, it would not have occurred without the network of international trade routes under British hegemony created by war capitalism. In this network, the products of Indian weavers were used to buy slaves in Africa, who were then forced to work on America's plantations in order to produce agricultural goods for European consumers.

This trade empire provided three essential preconditions for the Industrial Revolution. First, there was an enormous accumulation of capital in the hands of British merchants and financiers that could subsequently be invested in industrialization. Second, it opened an international market for English textiles from the start, without which factory production would not have been profitable. As early as 1800, two-thirds of English industrial production went to export. Third, it guaranteed cheap access to the crucial raw material for industrialization, i.e. cotton, initially from India, later from American slave plantations. In this way the exploding demand for cotton did not result in a significant price rise, which might have put an end to the dynamic of industrialization.

The state provides cheap labour

The role of the British state, however, was not restricted to the provision of a war fleet that could secure the supply of raw materials, trade routes, and slavery. Domestically, the state was also actively involved in industrialization, performing a wide range of tasks: the construction of roads and canals, and later of railroads and telephone lines; the legal protection of property rights and laws enabling the privatization of the commons, which uprooted parts of the rural population; the particularly brutal poor laws that refused any support to destitute families and punished begging in a draconian fashion; and the long period of suppression of attempts to organize trade unions.

All this ensured that industrialization had a cheap and constantly growing labour force for working in the "dark satanic mills". The state played an important role as well in the protectionist defense of the emerging English textile industry by way of a total ban on the importing of Indian textiles. Not until British manufacturers had achieved superiority over all other producers in the world did "free trade" become state doctrine.

Counter-program to the Washington Consensus

The Industrial Revolution was the exact counter-program to the current theses of neoliberalism and the Washington Consensus, with the help of which we keep poverty in less developed countries firmly in place. The British state during the Industrial Revolution was not a weak state, but a strong state more than willing to intervene in the economy by way of high taxes and debt. It was a state, moreover, that did not champion free trade but protectionist tariffs and the unconditional support of its own manufacturers, if necessary through war and military intervention.

Industrialization on the European continent and in the United States followed the same model. The cause of the Napoleonic Wars was not the permanent conflict with Prussia or the differences of opinion with Russian Tsar Alexander. The real cause was Napoleon's attempt to put in place a maritime blockade against English products on the European market in order to create the conditions for the emergence of an independent French industry. The blockade was continually subverted by Prussia as well as Russia. Napoleon's overthrow was therefore a serious setback for French industry.

Industrialization in Germany and in the United States took place behind high tariff walls and with massive state support. Polanyi points out that the creation of a national market in many countries was itself "the outcome of a conscious and often violent intervention on the part of government" and clearly not "the result of the gradual and spontaneous emancipation of the economic sphere from governmental control".[61]

Domination through free trade

For the same reason, militarily weaker states such as China or Japan in the nineteenth century were forced to sign treaties that committed them to refraining from protecting their economies with tariffs or trade barriers. As a result, they experienced very little industrialization of their own while existing trades, unable to compete with industrially manufactured imported goods, collapsed. China, for long periods one of the world's wealthiest countries, in the first half of the twentieth century was turned into a poorhouse with a level of economic performance per capita that in 1952 was lower than in 1820. Japan's and later China's economic development did not start until they ended free trade, adopting protectionist policies and state intervention for their own nascent industries following the model of the industrialized countries.

In the twentieth century, the significance of state subsidies, public spending on research, and military policy in the service of economic interests grew even further. One goal continues to be securing raw materials for the economy, from cotton in the eighteenth century to oil in the twentieth and twenty-first centuries, for which states are quite willing to employ their military apparatus. To this day, the global power status of the United States rests primarily on the particular brutality and ruthlessness with which it ensures access to crucial raw materials or markets, if necessary by military means.

However, the prosperity and economic dynamics of industrialized countries as well as of most emerging economies are in many other respects the result of state intervention. Many of us will clearly remember how states managed to mobilize trillions of dollars overnight in order to shore up their flagging banks. Since that time, the financial industry, in particular the large globally operating banks, enjoy cost-free state re-insurance, without which their business model of taking extreme risks with a minimum of their own capital would not work. And in other areas as well, the state ensures that profit, on the one hand, and risk and liability on the other, remain separate.

State innovation

The state is present in virtually all sectors of the economy in the form of credit and export guarantees, capital infusion, billions in subsidies, and publicly funded research, in particular in areas of innovation and the attainment or defense of technological dominance. From silicon-based semi-conductors and the Internet to GPS, from pathbreaking medical innovations to nanotechnology—it was not private firms but public research laboratories or taxpayer-funded development programs that produced the decisive breakthroughs.

In its early period, Silicon Valley was little more than a branch of the Pentagon. Firms settling around the military base in San José and the NASA research centre in Mountain View lived on the billions of dollars in orders for military goods during the Cold War. Many giants of the digital economy have their roots here, and they have all profited massively from state subsidies. Apple, for example, is anything but the successful project of independent entrepreneurs who worked their way up from garage workshop to global corporation. With significant funding from the government's SBIC program set up for innovative small firms, Apple has cleverly incorporated publicly financed technology into its own products.

Apple's government-funded technology

"As a matter of fact, there is not a single technology in the iPhone that was not publicly funded"[62], writes Italian-U.S. economist Mariana Mazzucato, who is Professor in the Economics of Innovation at the University of Sussex. She lists twelve key technologies on which the performance of iPods, iPads, and iPhones is based: microprocessors, microchips, micro hard drives, hard disk drivse, liquid crystal displays, lithium, polymer and lithium-ion batteries, digital signal processors, the Internet, http and HTML, cellular technology and networks, satellite navigation (GPS), the click wheel, multi-touch screens, and language recognition technology SIRI. All of these technologies were developed with public funding and under state authority.

Mazzucato reminds us that the algorithm behind Google's success was devised by people who at the time were living on funds from the public National Science Foundation; that the molecular antibodies forming the foundation of the biotechnology industry were discovered in the laboratories of the state Medical Research Council (MRC) in the UK; and that in general the most innovative young enterprises in the United States were and are financed by public funds, such as the program Small Business Innovation Research (SBIR), rather than private venture capital.

The pharmaceutical industry in most countries, and especially in the United States, is highly subsidized as well. The U.S. National Institutes of Health annually invest more than 30 billion dollars in medical research, with the results of which private pharmaceutical companies can then add to their profits. Ever since registering private patents for results of publicly financed research was legalized, this model has been particularly lucrative.

Risk-averse capital

Private capital really is a timid creature. It shuns risk and is rarely in for the long haul. Sectors with high uncertainty and long time horizons—which in the case of genuine innovation is always the case—are avoided until the breakthrough is tangible. Private venture capital usually does not come on board until an initial public offering or the sale of the enterprise appears realistic within a period of 5–10 years. Where true uncertainty is predominant since possibilities are still being explored and tested while prospects as well as commercial applications are simply unknown, either the state will act as financier or new ideas won't have a chance. The innovation process in the private sector is focused on improvements, refinements, and the further development of existing processes and products—and even here, as we have seen, with an increasingly short time horizon.

Blind faith in the market and growing public debt have resulted in a significant reduction of state activities globally. This is also true with respect to research and innovation. As public funds have dried up, unsurprisingly the innovation dynamics of the economy has declined, at least as far as basic innovations are concerned.

"Small potatoes from Silicon Valley"

An article entitled "Small potatoes from Silicon Valley" in the German business daily *Handelsblatt* discussed the question why so few revolutionary inventions were made in the United States. The author states that in terms of GDP, the country spends as much on R&D as it did in the 1960s. However, the composition of expenditure has changed. "In the 1960s the state accounted for two-thirds of total spending, while the private sector contributed one-third. The proportion has since reversed." According to the author, this is precisely the problem since the direction of state-funded research is necessarily different than that of private enterprise. "The state has much greater staying power. ... Enterprises have a more short-term time horizon, searching for improved technology that has a rapid payoff. ... Notwithstanding all the glamour of Silicon Valley, the high time of innovation in the United States was from 1950 to 1970. At that time the rate of productivity growth was almost twice as high as it was between 1990 and 2010 ...".

Due to a lack of public funding, little work is being done on transformative technologies, i. e. those that would represent genuine breakthroughs and are needed, for instance, to solve our energy problems. Instead incremental technologies, partial improvements, or even fake technologies have become of primary concern, i. e. technologies that do not create any added value but nevertheless can somehow be sold. The *Handelsblatt* article mentions as a positive exception among others the National Institutes of Health, where big budgets still in fact finance research into genuine innovations.[63]

In Europe, where the establishment has an even stronger tendency actually to believe in the theories of the economic mainstream rather than just using them as a convenient justification in the pursuit of their own interests, the situation is even more hopeless. This is not due to a lack of funds. The European Central Bank is printing trillions in order to propel the financial markets from one bubble to the next and to further inflate the wealth of the richest 1 percent. The idea, on the other hand, to invest these funds in a serious innovation offensive—from energy to health—is so foreign to officials that it doesn't even play a secondary role.

Industry calling for government support

German corporations often bemoan the fact that the German state fails to take serious initiatives with respect to innovation. The usual effusive praise for the market as the superior form of organization is seldom heard in this context. In 2012, Reinold Achatz, the former head of global research at Siemens and current director of the working group "Value-added oriented innovation strategies" at the Federation of German Industry, presented a paper with representatives of

Volkswagen, RWE, Bayer, EADS, BASF and other German corporations calling for significantly more state initiative.

They warned that otherwise, important parts of value-added activity would leave Germany. They argued that the fundamental changes anticipated until 2030 in transportation, genetics, nanotechnology, IT, and communications technology as well as energy supply could be accomplished only with active state support. According to industry representatives, individual corporations "may themselves no longer be able ... to implement crucial innovations in the market"[64]. (This is particularly the case, one might add, if Siemens fails to implement innovative ideas that do not promise a return of at least 16 percent...) The state is called upon to do the job of advancing research into innovative technologies with billions in taxpayer funds, thus protecting large corporations from the risk of failure. In addition, the government is asked to work as a "catalyst", facilitating cooperation between enterprises from different sectors.

Anti-government rhetoric as the job of neoliberal ideologues

Anti-government rhetoric and market euphoria are the job of market ideologues. When one's own business interests are concerned, the government can be surprisingly helpful. Since the corporations' earlier appeal for government support had not received sufficient attention from politicians, Dieter Schweer, another representative of the Federation of German Industry, repeated the call for help three years later. In view of the meagre representation of German firms in the Internet and communication sectors, he pleaded: "We need stronger state support for private investment in research and development."[65] Whether there should be a larger share for the public in the resulting profits was of course not discussed.

Economic freedom in capitalism therefore does not consist in keeping the state out. Rather, it consists in utilizing the state in such a way that it relieves corporations as much as possible from risk and liability, finances their research, subsidizes their ventures, and in general fights for their interests domestically and internationally. Even if, with the kind cooperation of Dublin, Luxembourg, or Delaware, the corporations in return deprive the state of a growing share of taxes on profits.

5. WHY GENUINE ENTREPRENEURS DO NOT NEED CAPITALISM

What is capitalism? The question may not be as trivial as it sounds. Up to this point, the present book has explained that capitalism is clearly not what it is normally taken to be. It is not a market economy, at least not in the sense that real competition and open markets represent the crucial control mechanisms in economic life. It is not a meritocratic society, since the highest incomes are the returns from capital ownership, which are not based on personal performance. It is also not an economic order in which effort and commitment determine career outcomes and success. Even in society's middle, individual status is once again for the most part a matter of family background as well as chance and luck, while at the very top, family and inheritance have always been decisive. Also, capitalism is not an economy in which private actors make large profits for taking particularly high personal risks. Rather, in a market structure in which a few corporations are dominant, while few if any opportunities exist for newcomers, the highest profits are achieved where risk tends to be low. What is more, the state supports corporations in a variety of ways, shielding their owners from a large part of the risk.

But if capitalism is not what it is usually seen to be, what then is it? In short, capitalism is distinguished from other economic orders by the fact that *capital* is not merely used for production, but *for the sake of capital*, that is, that the essential goal of production is the return on invested capital. Products are not manufactured in response to existing needs or in order to create employment, but rather as a way of exploiting the invested capital by extracting the highest possible profit. Wages are a cost factor, customers a means to an end, profit is the goal, with the payout of this profit taking the form of capital income. And because only monetary return is at stake, the same capital owner may invest in firms in any sector of the economy, or move from one to the other.

5.1 Entrepreneurs without profit

Incomes unrelated to performance on the one hand, and open markets and free competition on the other, do not match. Mainstream economics, which assumes that we live in an economy with functioning markets, genuine competition, and open access to capital, has always had problems explaining the existence of stable profits and capital incomes.

In a functioning market, firms are able to make short-term profits by offering a new product or service that has not been offered by anyone else, or by entering a market in which demand outstrips supply. At that moment, they control a temporary monopoly which, however, competitors will soon crack. In the long run, tough competition in an open market means there is no reason why an entrepreneur should receive more than what his own entrepreneurial performance generates.

Marx's profit theory

According to Marx, profits in capitalism are based on the worker creating more value with his work than the value his labour has on the capitalist market. The capitalist buys labour power and sells the product of work and, since the two differ, he is taking a cut without violating the laws of equal exchange. This theory accurately describes the foundation of profit, namely that those in dependent employment generate more than they are being paid for, i. e. that a part of the product of labour accrues to the firm's owner. But this doesn't answer the question why this should be the case.

If it was a natural law that the value of labour and thus wages were always lower than the value of the products made, the solution would be evident: Workers, become self-employed, hire your wife, son, and cousin while you're at it, and cash in on the profits that the capitalist has always kept for himself. The problem with this model is that things don't work this way.

Of course there are many former employees who have set up their own businesses or were pushed into self-employment. The more skilled and sophisticated the job they do, and the smaller the number of people who can do this job, and the greater their chance of earning a decent income as a self-employed person. The more basic the work and the larger the competition from others offering the same thing, the more precarious the situation tends to be. Even if the person setting up a small cafe or starting a creative online service has used all her savings, people will not be lining up to pay her a return. The young entrepreneur can usually be satisfied if she somehow manages to cover the interest for the bank loan. In highly competitive markets, earnings are rarely significantly higher than a normal wage for a comparable job, and often it is less. It's not a way to get rich. What are people doing wrong?

The textbook world: not a healthy biotope

In fact, we should pose the question the other way around. Why do regular profits and capital income without work exist in the first place? This is not a trivial question, since—at least in an efficient market—no one should be receiving anything without providing something in return.

Let's start with profits, since in order to distribute capital income, a firm has to generate profits first, and not just sporadically but regularly. Profits—particularly in excess of immediate investment needs—obviously exist only in the absence of sufficient competition.

There may be a variety of reasons for this. One way is to distinguish yourself from your competitors through higher quality and continuous product innovation, or by occupying a market niche with a high-tech product that cannot simply be copied. This route is followed by firms that are called "hidden champions", which in terms of sales do not belong to the big players but usually realize large profits. Another way is to establish yourself in a saturated market that on account of high capital requirements or government-protected patents and copyrights is closed to new entrants. This is the route followed by the large industrial corporations.

Thus there are a variety of ways in which competition can be eliminated or at least restricted. Some of these—such as specializing in a particularly sophisticated product—may well be in the public interest. Others—such as the takeover of competing firms or the exploitation of patents as an instrument to block competition—are not. However, regardless of the means employed, the important point is that in capitalist production, competition occurs only in a limited fashion. If, on the other hand, the economy is working along the lines described in standard economics textbooks—many suppliers competing with a standard product having little influence on the market price, while new firms are established all the time, putting pressure on existing enterprises—this is not a suitable environment for capitalism to thrive in. In sectors with conditions like these, there may well be successful individual entrepreneurs who achieve a decent income for their performance. But such businesses rarely produce regular profits and capital incomes without work.

Keeping competition at bay

We have described the situation in the chapter on "robber barons"— the merchant of the early period who invested his capital in long-distance trade and enjoyed high returns, benefiting above all from limited competition. Long-distance trade was open only to those who were able to raise the large sums of capital needed for long trade routes. The merchant's own capital was extended through loans and bank bills, but they were available only those who already had wealth. Thus only very few individuals had the wherewithal to engage in these projects, and this small group monopolized the connection between producer and buyer. It was a profitable business.

Large-scale manufacturing is an ideal environment for capitalism. Its typical market form since the late nineteenth century is the oligopoly: a market dominated by a small number of large producers with relatively stable market shares in which new entrants are rarely able to upset the business of the established actors. This is a rich soil for consistently high profits, which can then be distributed in the form of incomes without work.

In the service sector, capitalism has taken root where similar conditions exist: a small number of large companies, limited competition, closed markets. The digital economy is a particularly favourable environment in this respect since it has a tendency not only towards developing stable oligopolies but monopolies of exclusive producers. As we have seen, it is not just the extreme advantages of size—once an application has been programmed, copies are virtually free—but also the network effect. Once established as an industry standard, it becomes virtually impossible to dislodge.

5.2 "Competition and capitalism are a contradiction in terms"

If you want to maintain stable profits, you should ensure that your firm has as few competitors as possible. Whether the competition is kept at bay through superior quality and innovation power or through patent rights and other state privileges, through simple economies of scale and high capital requirements or through digital network effects is of considerable importance for society. For the enterprise itself it is secondary, but the more convenient and popular of these methods for keeping competitors at a safe distance are economically the most damaging.

In any event, the previously quoted founder of PayPal and Silicon Valley billionaire, Peter Thiel, is correct when he writes: "Actually, capitalism and competition are opposites. Capitalism is premised on the accumulation of capital, but under perfect competition all profits get competed away."[66] It follows in short that "competition and capitalism are a contradiction in terms."[67] This is true. However, in contrast to what Thiel has in mind this is not an argument against competition, but an argument against capitalism.

Monopoly price for capital

This explains how stable profits are generated. But why are there capital incomes without something in return? Conceivably profits could remain in the enterprise and be reinvested. As we have seen, capital incomes do not represent any remuneration for delayed consumption since capital is not generated by delayed consumption and saving. Nor do capital incomes represent remuneration for any kind of work, since while capital is generated by labour, it is not the labour of those who own the capital. Invoking the risk taken by the capital owner is not a valid argument either, since risk is undoubtedly higher for young start-ups than for the shareholders of an established corporation.

The most frequent justification is that only thanks to capital providers is it possible for entrepreneurs to set up firms and for workers to work—at least in all those sectors in which capital requirements are far above the life savings of an average earner. This argument does indeed go to the heart of the matter. Capital incomes, which today account for almost a third of our economic output, emerge only because the large majority of people in our current economic order do not, and never will, have any direct access to capital.

In the second part of the book, we will show that this does not necessarily have to be the case and that an economy in which access to capital is democratized would be significantly more innovative and dynamic than the present economy. Under current conditions, however, unearned capital incomes are simply the monopoly price we have to pay, since the existing ownership system is concentrating capital in the hands of a small minority of society.

Savings are no longer scarce, on the contrary—in Western economies they exist in abundance, while banks pay basically no interest to savers. However, capital is scarce, and those who control it make fundamental decisions on investments and jobs. This is why capital continues to earn substantial returns.

"... giving up autonomy"

In our economy, of course there are not only profit hunters who see firms simply as lucrative investment objects—there are also many genuine entrepreneurs. They are those who work together with their employees for a dynamic economy, innovation, and quality products. However, the assumption that entrepreneurs need capitalism is a major error. Precisely because access to capital is difficult, it holds firms back and makes life difficult for them.

Schumpeter already noticed that in many firms, there was a conflict of interest between entrepreneurs and capital investors. Obviously the individual establishing a firm needs purchasing power, i.e. capital, in order to be able to invest. Unless he hails from a wealthy family, the entrepreneur will not himself have the requisite financial means, which is why "for him ... private ownership of the means of production [becomes] an obstacle"[68], as Schumpeter emphasized. For a new entrepreneur from a less wealthy background has to secure the capital he needs from others. Even if he succeeds, which quite often is not the case, he ends up in a position of dependence, since the capital investors as rightful owners are entitled to exert direct influence over the firm.

"... and I'm supposed to give up my autonomy and stand by while others take charge"[69], complained the engineer Gottlieb Daimler, who together with Wilhelm Maybach had built the first high-speed gasoline engine and the first four-wheeled vehicle with an internal combustion engine, when he had to accept the industrialists Dutten-hofer and Lorenz as co-owners of the Daimler Motor Company. The history of many firms is a history of highly talented technicians and courageous founders who, upon bringing in external investors, lost their autonomy, subsequently wasting their energy on problems and conflicts with co-owners. In quite a few cases such conflicts ended with the actual technological head and founder leaving the firm in frustration.

Motivated by filthy lucre

The Person behind the Product is the title of a book portraying 40 successful engineers and firm founders who created the foundation for Germany's top listed corporations. The upshot of these portraits is summarized as follows: "With their inventions inventors frequently lost their independence. They often had to rely on what today is called risk capital. This was no different for the pioneers of motorization such as Nikolaus Otto, Gottlieb Daimler, or Karl Benz. They were forced to go through serious conflicts with the beneficiaries of their patents, i. e. the investors."[70]

While these were portraits of entrepreneurs from the late nineteenth and early twentieth centuries, the U.S. economist and head of the Foundation on Economic Trends, Jeremy Rifkin, describes the same situation for the present. "[M]any entrepreneurs I've met over the years are far more driven by the creative act than the almighty dollar. The pecuniary fetish generally comes later when entrepreneurial enterprises mature, become publicly traded in the market, and take on shareholders whose interest is in the return on their investment. There are countless tales of entrepreneurs driven out of their own companies by professional management brought in to transform the enterprise from a creative performance to a sober, "financially responsible" business, a euphemism that means focusing more attention on the bottom line."[71] We could also say: those welcomed aboard to transform a creative enterprise into a capitalist one.

Recipe for inequality

For good reasons, most economists interested in competition, economic dynamism, the meritocratic principle, and prosperity have not had a favourable view of capitalism. The classical liberal economist Alexander Rüstow lamented "the quasi-theological absolutized laissez-faire degenerate subsidized-monopolistic-protectionist-pluralist economy of the nineteenth and twentieth centuries we call 'capitalist' and 'capitalism'", which was entirely different from "the free market economy of perfect competition, the normal subject of liberal economic theory."[72]

"With the intention of doing God's will, the devil was given free rein, the devil of seeking enrichment at the expense of others, lust for power, and the will to dominate."[73]

Ludwig Erhard wrote about his teacher, the economist Franz Oppenheimer: "He recognized capitalism as the institution that results in inequality, indeed enshrines inequality, even though he was certainly not interested in simple-minded egalitarianism. On the other hand, he despised communism since it necessarily destroyed freedom. He called for a new way—a third way—a happy synthesis that would provide a solution."[74]

Genuine entrepreneurs have no need for capitalism. With the disappearance of capitalism, the exclusivity of access to capital could be eliminated, and with it the opportunity to turn other people's labour into one's own income without work.

PART II

MARKET ECONOMY INSTEAD OF ECONOMIC FEUDALISM: SKETCH OF A MODERN ECONOMIC ORDER

[T]here is nothing more difficult to take in hand, more perilous to conduct, or more uncertain in its success, than to take the lead in the introduction of a new order of things, because the innovator has for enemies all those who have done well under the old conditions, and lukewarm defenders in those who may do well under the new. This coolness arises partly from fear of the opponents, who have the laws on their side, and partly from the incredulity of men, who do not readily believe in new things until they have had a long experience of them.

Machiavelli, The Prince (1532)[75]

6. WHAT MAKES US RICH?

It is baffling to what extent the dominant faith in the market keeps us from even posing certain questions. What is it really that makes a society productive, creative, innovative, and prosperous? And what incentives and power relations lead to diminishing wealth and economic decline? What economic framework do we need for a good life, and what conditions stand in our way?

Many of us have given up reflecting on the rationality of our social institutions. According to the dominant article of faith, whatever the market generates is efficient, otherwise it would not have come into existence. Yet, as we have seen in the preceding chapters, our economic life is rarely the result of spontaneous market decisions. We feel we are ruled by anonymous markets, while failing to notice that powerful economic interests have been in charge for a long time.

6.1 The social order is of our own making

Our property law, our monetary order, and our currency system are institutions that have come into being as a result of political decisions—or non-decisions. They have not always existed. Over the past few decades they have in part changed dramatically, most recently under the influence of new digital technologies. Of course we are free to design these institutions in a different way if we conclude that they don't work in their present form and that they benefit a small minority while short-changing a large majority. Since they are man-made, we do not have to accept these institutions as they are.

Institutional change starts with the realization that institutions can be changed. Each of us now has the right to transfer with the push of a button a million euros from their bank account to Singapore or Panama, or to buy shares on Wall Street. This has not always been the case. Is this right, which most people will never exercise in the course of their lives, really so sacrosanct that we are willing to put up with the many downsides of the free flow of capital, such as large-scale tax evasion and the vulnerability of states to blackmail? Wouldn't it be much more important to have a financial system in which every qualified entrepreneur has access to capital?

Forgotten civilization

The history of humankind has always known both periods of general prosperity motivating the spirit of innovation, improving production techniques, and significantly raising the standard of living for a large number of people, as well as periods in which great civilizations broke up, newly developed technical knowledge was forgotten, and life once again became harder, more hopeless, and poorer. The best-known example for the rise and decline of great systems is the history of the Roman Empire from its beginnings several hundred years before the start of the Christian calendar to its end between the fifth and seventh centuries. Indian cultures, ancient Egypt and Greece had similar, if more short-lived, experiences. China experienced several ages of prosperity and subsequent decline.

Wars and civil wars frequently destabilized societies, thus causing economic decline. It is not difficult to see why. The more people's lifetimes are wasted on military service, and thus for destruction rather than for production and trade, the poorer a society will be. If wars or civil wars continue for extended periods, insecurity grows and investment in larger projects will come to a halt. Dangerous transport routes impair trade or destroy it altogether. Technologies that are profitable only on large scales will no longer be produced. Since they are no longer used, they will eventually be forgotten.

After the fall of the Roman Empire, its European network of roads fell into disuse, cities declined, farmers returned to subsistence production, mansions were replaced by huts and castles. Only a tiny minority learned how to read and write. Contemporary examples of countries that had attained a respectable level of development with good health and education systems but were ruined by wars and civil wars can be found in the Middle East and North Africa. Iraq and Syria belong to this group, as does Libya. These countries have by now lost almost all their former prosperity.

Exclusive decline

However, there is also the opposite phenomenon—decline in times of peace, precisely as a result of stability. The U.S. economist Mancur Olson was the first to investigate this phenomenon, and it is at the centre of his theory of the rise and decline of nations. Olson's point of departure is the thesis that small social groups with similar interests are better able to organize themselves than larger ones. Since the upper class of a society is a relatively small group, it is also particularly well organized and networked. This holds all the more true the more stable a system is over a long period of time.

Since people who are doing well would like to preserve this state of affairs and preserve it for their children, privileged sectors of society always have an interest in securing their position in a way that makes it as independent as possible from actual performance, and in this form pass it on to their offspring. This is why at the top continuing stability gives rise to what Olson calls an "exclusive distributional coaltion". Social rules are made that prevent those who are not already part of the self-appointed elite from joining this exclusive group. The hereditary principle of the nobility is such a rule, as are ownership rights that restrict access to capital primarily to heirs.

Of course *exclusive* institutions don't emerge only for the protection of the upper class. They also exist in other sectors. What is crucial is really only that a relatively small interest group has sufficient power in society to refuse outsiders access to the sector in which they earn their living, and if possible to provide for the privileged access of their own offspring. *Exclusive institutions* thus do not reward skills and performance, but descent and blood relations. Ultimately, the goal is always the elimination of potential competitors and the securing of incomes without work. Not only antiquity and the feudal age, but capitalism as well, as we have seen, were and are in many sectors based on exclusive structures. If these structures come to dominate societies, their economies become sluggish and inflexible because opportunities for creativity and talent are closed to a large part of the population.

The selection of the Mandarins

Inclusive institutions, according to Olson, are the exact opposite. They are open to everyone as long as they have the requisite talent and knowledge. An inclusive society thus would be one in which every true talent can make it to the very top, irrespective of social class. In its pure form such a society has never existed, but the closer the ideal can be approximated, the better the society will be off because it will be able to make full use of its creative and intellectual potential.

Ancient China had one of its golden ages during the Ming Dynasty between the fourteenth and seventeenth centuries. A major characteristic of this time was the selection system for higher state offices, the Mandarins. Whereas in Europe at that time political leadership positions were simply inherited, the positions of the Mandarins were in principle open to everyone. Applying for this office required passing a complicated examination system, and whoever did best among hundreds of applicants got the job. As historian Fernand Braudel notes, as a result of this system, for the offspring of poorer classes top positions in the Chinese state bureaucracy were "in any event significantly more accessible than the large Western universities as late as the nineteenth century."[76] The result was not only social mobility but, above all, a higher quality of public administration.

The Venetian *commenda*

The golden age of the trading city of Venice was also related to career opportunities that were unusual for the time. They were based on a specific legal form of commercial firm that opened a road to the top for enterprising young men who did not come from wealthy families and had no capital of their own. This legal form, the *commenda*, was a partnership set up by two merchants for the purpose of a trade mission. What was special about this arrangement was that only one of the two had to contribute capital. While the capital investor as the financier of the project stayed in Venice, the other partner accompanied the cargo and lived through the dangers and uncertainties of the long trip. If the project was a success, the travelling merchant received 25 percent of the profit. If he had contributed himself a small sum to the project up front, the profit was often equally divided between the two.

The *commenda* ensured that on the historical lists of the Venetian upper class from the years 960, 971, and 982, a majority were new names. On the downside, of course, families from the old elite were displaced and could not pass on their privileged position to their children. This did not sit well with those who had made it to the top. The Venetian nobility eventually decided to transform itself into a hereditary nobility open only its own descendants. The *commenda* was outlawed. Subsequently, the old established elites once again had exclusive control over lucrative trading routes, no longer sharing their profits with anyone. This turning point was recorded in history under the name of *serrata*, the "closure".

Einstein as farm labourer

For the community, such *closures* always meant losses in wealth. It is not difficult to understand that a society in which anyone can become a physicist will have better physicists than one in which only a small group will be instructed in basic mathematical and physical knowledge. In the latter case there is a much greater danger that an Einstein will not be recognized and end up as a farm labourer. And naturally a society in which in principle anyone can become an entrepreneur if they have the skills and good ideas will have the better entrepreneurs compared to a society in which such activities are open only to a few due to a lack of generally accessible start-up financing. In this respect, the capitalist system is guilty of an immense waste of creativity and talents. Without sufficient capital, even the best entrepreneurs will frequently end in failure—unless they were smart enough from the start not to try to set up an enterprise.

As we have seen, capitalism in the industrialized countries during its golden years, i. e. in the decades following World War II, created career opportunities for many, even if they never made it to the very top. The enormous dynamism of this period is closely related to the openness and permeability of social institutions. One key was the democratization of education all the way to the university level. Equally important was the existence of many well-paid positions in the public sector as well as in the private economy that could be attained even without access to capital. Only the latter continued to be largely reserved for the upper class.

Modern illiterates

This is now history. Today children from the poorer sections of society grow up without higher education, in part even without elementary skills in mathematics, reading, and writing. Many do not have a command of their own mother tongue, but possess only a minimal vocabulary with which, untroubled by the rules of grammar, they cobble together incomplete sentences. Such deficits can be easily corrected during Kindergarten and elementary school. However, it cannot be done in a chronically underfunded education system that is short on everything from the number of teachers to modern teaching technology. If this is not addressed, the job opportunities of young people who cannot even speak properly seem a foregone conclusion.

For reasons of social justice as well as for economic reasons, a modern economic order should create institutions that ensure that children's opportunities depend as little as possible on their social environment and as much as possible on their own abilities. The primary prerequisite is an education system that makes it possible to discover such talents in the first place. Since the European Enlightenment, the meritocratic idea of performance-driven career opportunities as opposed to feudal privileges and inherited prerogatives has been a basic demand. It has not been fulfilled to this day.

One part of the answer to the question of what makes a society prosperous is this: societies will be the wealthier the better they use their creative and intellectual potential. Exclusive institutions are obstacles in this respect. Since, in the long run, any stable society has a tendency to give rise to such institutions, a conscious effort is necessary to erect barriers against attempts at closing off privileged terrain.

Labour-saving progress

But this is only half the truth. Obviously, social creativity can be unleashed and directed at hideous goals. The atom bomb was invented by creative minds as well. Not all technological progress is desirable, some of it is destroying the basis of our lives. What are the technologies and innovations that really make it possible for us to have a better life? And what are the economic incentives we need in order to focus invention talents on such steps forward?

Evidently material welfare is not dependent on how much money we have in the bank but on what we can buy with our money. We can buy what our economy produces in a certain period of time, which in turn depends on the technologies being applied. In agriculture this is self-evident. As long as we tilled our fields with horse-drawn wooden ploughs, a large segment of the population had to live on and work the land, since otherwise society would have simply starved. Nowadays, based on modern technology, an individual farmer can work 100 hectares of land, guaranteeing the food supply of half a small city. Most people are therefore free to deal with other things. Without this kind of technological progress, industrialization could never have occurred.

In the industrial sector, the same process was repeated. While in the 1880s the cheapest bicycle cost an average worker in France or Germany six months' wages—which obviously meant that he couldn't afford it—by 1910 production costs had declined so much that one month's wage was enough. Today an average earner works less than a week for an inexpensive bicycle. Cars too did not become a mass product until people with regular incomes could earn the amount in a manageable period of time. While in 1908 in the United States about 4,700 hours at average wages were necessary to be able to afford a standard model, the value of a mid-range car today is about 1,000 hours.

The decisive factor underlying these price drops is the application of labour-saving technology. The production of most goods today requires much less work effort than one or even two centuries ago—just as every loaf of bread we eat today contains much less labour than in previous times. Labour saving means that we can produce more or different things in the same time. This is a major reason why we live better today than our ancestors. In this sense we could say: an economy makes us wealthier if it motivates us to apply labour-saving processes, as well as to discover and supply new useful goods or services.

There has to be an appropriate environment for people to come up with innovations, new labour-saving methods or new products. And there need to be incentives for new ideas to be applied in the economy. This may sound trivial but it isn't. Economic history is rich in inventions that arrived too early or in the wrong environment, which is why they disappeared in the archives.

The steam engine, for instance, was based on principles known since Archimedes. But why should the Greeks or Romans have built such engines if they had slaves who worked for them, pretty much for free. In 1313 the Chinese Wang Zhen described a "machine for the spinning of hemp fibre" that came pretty close to the spinning jenny and the water frame, the most important machines of the industrial revolution. He was not successful; no one built and used his machine. In England, in 1589, one William Lee constructed a knitting machine that would have made the manufacturing of textiles much more productive, i. e. less labour-intensive. He presented the machine to Elizabeth I. The queen of England was not pleased, for the reason that such mechanization would have horrendous consequences for those whose livelihood depended on the manufacturing of wool by arduous manual labour. Only with capitalism would such reservations come to be ignored.

The profit calculus is a strong incentive to apply labour-saving technology and to bring new products and services to market. Whoever produces something novel that no one else supplies will, if successful, realize large profits. The same applies to those who make products similar to those of others, but on account of a new technology do so more cheaply. The enormous advances in productivity of the past two centuries and the inexhaustible wealth of ideas in the discovery of new things are by and large based on this basic motivation. As a result, more and more work came to be done by machines and devices, while society as a whole became richer.

Faltering engine of innovation

To be sure, this capitalist engine of innovation works only within the limitations discussed in earlier chapters. Within firms, the innovation process requires well-equipped development departments. If the firms have shareholders on their backs who would rather see the money in their bank accounts, the innovation dynamic may come to a halt for this reason alone. If, in a firm, a radically new technology is discovered that might reduce the value of the capital invested and perhaps even call into question its entire business model, the most likely response will be to keep the inventions under locks. An engineer of the Eastman Kodak Company, at the time the global leader in the production of films and cameras with the old analogue technology, is said to have invented the first digital camera as early as 1975. The firm filed the unwelcome innovation—until others started to market it.

Fundamental innovations are therefore most successful in new enterprises. However, if there is a lack or shortage of start-up capital, the dynamic will stop. Patent law is another way by which the economic application of innovations may be postponed for many years.

Cheap labour, low investment

A serious impediment for the use of labour-saving technologies are schemes to lower the cost of labour, which can ultimately make production even cheaper than adopting a more modern technology. It was no coincidence that the German neoliberal reform package Agenda 2010 went hand in hand with a massive reduction in private sector investment. Part of the reason was that through temporary work, contracts, and other modifications the average cost of labour was cut, which significantly reduced the payoff of investments in labour-saving technology.

This applies even more forcefully on the global scale. In this context, the dynamic is self-reinforcing. Low-wage countries are generally less innovative than high-wage countries. Of course countries manufacturing for the most part non-innovative standard products are faced with much greater competition, which is also why they cannot afford to pay higher wages. In the context of high-tech products, on the other hand, talk about wage competition as a rule is a front for other considerations. Firms manufacturing things that Romania or Bangladesh can't produce do not need to worry about the wage levels in those countries.

6.2 How do ideas emerge?

An innovative economy has to provide incentives for the development of new technologies and products and for their commercialization. Let's begin by focusing on the first point. What is the best environment for ideas and inventions to emerge? Since no other economic order has generated as many innovations as capitalism, the standard theory is that inventions are made because there is an opportunity to commercialize them, which in turn promises large profits. The typical inventor would therefore be the amateur working out of his garage, who subsequently sets up an enterprise, concluding his life as a billionaire. In this context, the argument is made that patents and copyrights are of such importance because they alone secure the economic return on his ideas for the inventor.

The fallacy of this theory is that it describes the exception rather than the rule. In his excellent book *Where Good Ideas Come From*[77], U.S. author Steven Johnson examines the conditions under which the 200 most important innovations and scientific breakthroughs of the past 600 years were made. He distinguishes four main types of inventions: innovations made by a small circle of people within a firm or by an individual inventor, he classified as "individual". Innovations developed by a larger group with several teams and a division of tasks are referred to as "networked". With respect to both "individual" and "networked" innovations, he distinguishes between those that were developed from the start for commercial purposes and those that were not. Innovations developed on the basis of such motives fall under the heading of "market-oriented". In contrast, anything developed simply out of passion or enthusiasm is referred to as "not market-oriented".

Johnson's classification is thus composed of four categories, or in a graphic representation, four quadrants. The first category or quadrant contains "individual" and "market-oriented" innovations, i.e. everything developed by small firms and individual entrepreneurs. The second quadrant, "networked" and "market-oriented", includes technological breakthroughs that emerged from the research sections of large enterprises or from inter-firm cooperation with commercial goals. The third quadrant is populated by "individual" and "not market-oriented" lone wolves, i.e. individual thinkers, amateur scientists, and hobbyists who are not after big money but rather recognition from others to whom they are happy to give their ideas. Finally, the fourth quadrant of "networked" and "not market-oriented" innovations encompasses everything developed in academic and open source environments, i.e. in large cooperative networks in which ideas are constantly elaborated and improved.

Intellectual commons

It is widely assumed that for the most part, innovations show up in the first quadrant, i.e. under the rubrics of "individual" and "market-oriented". That would appear to be the typical capitalist mode of technological progress. Johnson shows, however, that reality is quite different. In the early beginnings of capitalism in the seventeenth and eighteenth centuries, most innovations were developed in a more academic environment rather than in a commercial environment. The great minds of this era—Newton, Franklin, Priestley, Hooke, Jefferson, Locke, Lavoisier, Linné—did not keep their ideas locked up for the purpose of commercial use, but they did whatever they could to spread them and make them available to others for further investigation and development.

True, even in this period there were a number of market-oriented inventions, though on the whole less by individuals than by larger groups. Frequently, the phenomenon of multiple invention has occurred: the same thing is discovered simultaneously by different people. A steam engine was constructed not only by James Watt but also by others. The reason is that such inventions rest on the accumulated knowledge of many creative minds. Then, at some point, the time has come for such a breakthrough. As Johnson concludes, "most of the key technologies that powered the Industrial Revolution were instances of what scholars call 'collective invention'."[78]

For the capitalist epoch proper, i. e. the time from the beginning of the nineteenth century to the present, Johnson's classification is even more to the point. The first quadrant, i. e. that of individual market-oriented innovation, once again has the fewest cases. For every lone wolf who in his own lab devises a patent-protected innovation, there are a half dozen collective inventions that were developed either by the development departments of large firms and networks of firms, or even more likely in the market-removed environment of the university or other public research institutions, i. e. on intellectual commons. In the end, Johnson arrives at the unequivocal conclusion that "competition turns out to be less central to the history of good ideas than we generally think."[79]

Legal walls

There are a number of reasons for this. To start with, great ideas mature best through exchange, openness, and communication—something that patents and copyrights tend to discourage if not rule out. Of course there are also forms of competition in the academic environment, e.g. for the number of citations as well as recognition and top positions. What does not exist are legal walls that protect ideas from further development and improvement by others. Researchers that constantly have to keep in mind legal questions will not be able to give full attention to their work. If development has to occur around the licensing rights of others, progress will be slowed down or made impossible unless it happens on the initiative of the patent owner. Since a research or development project may quickly violate the patents of others, there will also be increasing costs. This is all the more true since large enterprises are registering patents for the express purpose of creating obstacles for others.

Johnson refers to the Internet as an example. If its inventors had required licensing fees for any technology based on it, Tim Berners-Lee, programmer of HTML, would have probably never tried to create the World Wide Web. Especially since this was just a side project for which he had no funding. There are quite a few arguments in support of the view that an economy without patents would be more innovative and dynamic. The concern that without patents the motivation for the development of new technological developments would be lost is contradicted by the considerable development efforts made in many small and medium-sized enterprises that for reasons of cost never make it to patent registration. (If patent law actually *is* to provide exclusive temporary protection for genuinely individual ideas, it will have to be fundamentally redesigned.)

Fundamental scientific breakthroughs, as we have seen, are for the most part based on research in the public sphere rather than in the commercial world. To motivate such research does not require the prospect of future patent protection—the existence of commercial patents in fact creates problems and obstacles for such research. It is not necessary, but rather absurd, that private enterprises should be allowed to transform the results of publicly funded research into private ownership and patent rights.

High social costs

This creates high costs for society as a whole. In his book *The Conservative Nanny State*, U.S. author Dean Baker demonstrates this with respect to the pharmaceutical industry. According to recent figures, the industry has sales of 220 billion dollars in prescription drugs alone. Since prices for patent-protected drugs are more than three times those of generics, the public could save about 140 billion dollars a year if patent protection was eliminated. According to statistics by the pharmaceutical industry, their annual expenses for research into new drugs are about 41.1 billion dollars. Through higher prices for patent-protected drugs, the public thus pays 3 dollars for every dollar spent on research.

A considerable part of the development expenses of 41 billion dollars is so-called copycat research—i. e. drugs with a similar spectrum of actions as existing ones that are developed only because the original drugs are still under patent protection. Such expenses would be eliminated if patents did not exist. According to pharmaceutical firms, about two-thirds of all newly approved drugs are in this copycat category. These drugs therefore do not cure what existing ones could not. This is a significant waste of research funds. U.S. pharmaceutical corporations thus do not actually spend 41 billion dollars but only about 17 million on genuine drug innovation. And for these 17 billion in research expenses society pays 140 billion dollars as a result of increased prices, or an 8 dollar surcharge on every real research dollar. A pretty bad deal.

In addition to commercial spending, the United States annually allocates 30 billion dollars of public money to pharmaceutical research. Dean Baker offers the following simple calculation. If government were to eliminate patent protection while at the same time doubling public research spending on new drug development, this would more than make up for the current spending of the pharmaceutical industry. There would be no more need for research into duplicates. The 30 billion dollars in additional public spending would be offset by public savings of 140 billion dollars in lower prices as a result of the elimination of patent protection, and probably better results from pharmaceutical research. Who, other than the big pharma lobbyists with their tall tales, could object to embarking on such a route?

Planned innovation?

Since we are used to equating innovation with spontaneity and state activity with bureaucratic inertia, the idea of placing important areas of economic innovation under state authority may at first glance appear strange. It is true that innovation cannot be planned. Nevertheless, innovation has surprisingly frequently been promoted under state auspices and with public funding. Joseph Schumpeter, certainly no advocate of state intervention, in principle saw two ways of advancing innovative ideas and technologies. One is the innovative and creative individual entrepreneur who is driven by a desire to put his discovery to commercial use. The other is an innovation process that is based on the institutionalized cooperation of specialists.

In the earlier section on "the visible hand of the state", we saw that in the crucial technological breakthroughs of the past 150 years—from the railways to the Internet and nanotechnology—the state has always been involved, while the role of private enterprises was much smaller than is generally assumed. Especially fundamental innovations can be developed only in organized innovation systems that integrate basic research, applied research, and development and in which state institutions and public funding play a central role. Only the state is capable of financing research that does not have to pay off in the short term.

Fortune hunters and solar cells

Society can profit from these innovation processes only if it prevents the intellectual commons from being fenced in by private interests that transform publicly funded research results into private rights for the profit-making of large corporations and their shareholders. Of course innovations have to find their way into economic practice. Innovations need enterprises that apply them and turn them into a marketable product. But with viable innovative products, any well-managed enterprise can earn money even without patent rights, especially if the question of financing for young entrepreneurs is addressed more effectively than it currently is. It is therefore most important to facilitate the market success of innovations with start-up support for new enterprises, public loan guarantees, and state venture capital funds.

It is hard to imagine that the energy problem will be solved in other ways than by state initiative, since this will be a matter not only of technology but also the provision of new infrastructure. If the German government had used the 100 billion euros spent since the start of the new millennium on targeted research instead of on a failed energy reform, there might well be better storage technology and more efficient solar cells available now. At the same time, fewer fortune hunters would have exploited the allegedly green reform program.

Competition as a method of discovery

An innovative economy should achieve two goals. First, it should provide opportunities for creative individuals and facilitate the practical realization of their ideas if they are viable. Second, it should finance effective units for long-term research tasks and promote their commercialization through start-up support for young enterprises. "Competition as a method of discovery", as Hayek has poignantly described it, needs a place alongside a government-organized innovation process. There are after all different kinds of innovation. Solving the energy problem or a breakthrough in cancer research are challenges of a different order than making a joint-friendly running shoe, a kiss-proof lipstick, or a highly effective anti-pimple cream for teenagers.

This is not to say that the latter are unimportant. It is not only the major breakthroughs that make our lives better and more beautiful. Some large global corporations are in part based on inventions that appear banal, but that with respect to a specific problem have made life easier or more enjoyable. The entrepreneurial key to success of the pharmacist August Oetker was the idea to manufacture baking powder of consistent quality and package the exact amount necessary for a cake using 500 grams of flour. The inventor of gummy bears, Hans Riegel, rose to wealth with this innovation. And the chocolate manufacturer Rudolf Lindt once forgot to turn off his waterwheel-powered mixer, which made for an exceptionally creamy chocolate. For baking powder, gummy bears, or creamy chocolate, there is no need for state-funded research labs. But of course life would be poorer without them.

Innovations and ideas of this sort make the market irreplaceable. This is also the reason why an economic order with more real competition would be more prosperous and innovative than capitalism. If the role of markets was limited to the signalling effect of prices for supply and demand, the market economy as a model would soon become obsolete with the Internet of things and the digitally networked creation of value. In many sectors, "business on demand" is already standard practice—production does not respond to an anonymous market but to previously established demand.

However, with the deconcentration of corporations and improved start-up and financing opportunities for young enterprises, what functioning markets could do even better than today is making use of society's creative potential in the discovery of "minor" innovations—discovering market niches, improving existing products, refining labour-saving technologies, and experimenting with new ideas. No other mechanism provides as powerful a motivation for such achievements as free competition between many economic actors and the permanent openness of markets for new entrants. This is the field for private initiative and commercial activity.

7. HOW DO WE WANT TO LIVE?

We have grown accustomed to measuring a country's wealth primarily with one figure, the Gross Domestic Product, or GDP. The major goal of economic policy is to secure continuous growth in GDP. The higher this rate of growth, the more successful a government considers itself to be. According to this simple formula, our lives are improved by whatever gives a quick boost to our GDP.

However, there is an increasing recognition that there are problems with this simple measure. Not only are all incomes earned in a country simply added up, while their distribution is completely ignored. Also, GDP includes not only economic activities that do in fact improve our lives, but anything that an economy produces as long as it can be assigned a market price. A booming financial sector, excessive arms production, or growing drug consumption are examples of economic activities that push up GDP but do not make a society better off.

7.1 Tricky measure

Historically, reducing a country's economic performance to a single measure is a recent phenomenon. This measure was firmly established by the middle of the previous century, while its method of calculation was by no means self-explanatory but highly controversial. The inventor of the GDP formula, U.S. economist Simon Kuznets, was in favour of using private incomes as the basis for the calculation. However, ultimately a conception won out that was developed for the express purpose of concealing the welfare reduction resulting from sharply increased U.S. arms production before and during World War II.

The trick was that instead of giving primacy to net incomes, which do in fact determine the standard of living, production was put at the centre of the calculation. This measure makes no distinction between the production of tanks and the production of cars. We work with this construct to this day.

The claim here is not that the Gross Domestic Product as a measure of welfare is completely useless. We can assume that most people in a country with an annual per capita GDP of 30,000 dollars will be better off than those in a country with 3,000 dollars. To this extent, ending poverty in poor countries will certainly be related to GDP growth. However, in wealthy countries in recent years we have witnessed a simultaneous increase in GDP and poverty.

Our economy grows when more goods and services are produced and sold. We can produce more if either people work more—i.e. if unemployment declines or the population grows—or if on account of new technologies we can produce more in the same time. This fact alone demonstrates that growth cannot be an end in itself. While declining unemployment is desirable, longer working hours for those already in a full-time job are not. Similarly, producing more and more of the same thing will not necessarily improve our lives. The need for goods is finite, at some point it will be satisfied. Capitalist enterprises will always have an interest in *more* since that ensures *their* growth. But this will not necessarily increase *our* wealth.

The sleep of Australian aborigines

The creation of new things, products, and services that improve our lives and may even save resources—that is the meaning of real growth. This is why a categorical critique of growth is as erroneous as the belief that our supreme economic goal consists in producing ever growing quantities of what we already have. The purpose of labour-saving technologies is not to produce more of the same, say more cars and more refrigerators, with the same workforce. This may make a poor society wealthier, but in a wealthy society in which everybody owns a fridge and many own a car, it will not make for any significant gains. The welfare-enhancing effect of labour-saving advances is that society gains free time for other things—new products making life more pleasant, new services making life easier, or using more labour-intensive technologies in other sectors that are more sustainable, better for the environment or simply more humane. And let's not forget: labour-saving advances create room for spare time in which we can do what we want.

Older cultures were more careful in how they dealt with the lifetime gains of labour-saving innovations. The introduction of the steel axe in a group of Australian aborigines, the Yir Yoront, did not result in more extensive production but rather in longer periods of sleep. Books describing the blessings of growth and capitalism occasionally refer to this example as a particularly curious one: Look what idiots, just going to sleep instead of increasing their economic performance. What is so bad about getting more sleep? Many people with twelve or fourteen-hour workdays would probably welcome more rest. And newly-won spare time can of course be used in other ways than more sleep. If it is true that humans are social beings, any additional time we are able to spend with our loved ones will probably represent a greater gain in quality of life than a faster and more comfortable car.

Not always more, but always novel

Growing prosperity generally does not manifest itself in consuming more of the same, but in being able to afford things that previously were not in our shopping basket. Let's consider an example. A Michelin-starred restaurant is a rather labour-intensive and therefore expensive thing. The less time a society requires to produce all those things that make up the basics of modern life, the more starred restaurants it can afford to have. In other words, the more people will be able to afford going to such a restaurant.

Of course this is true only if technological progress really does benefit all, which under capitalist conditions is rather improbable. If the labour-saving innovation is not offset by quantitative growth, i. e. more cars or refrigerators, it often means for the affected workers that they lose their jobs and possibly experience a downgrading of their skills. If they do not find a new job with a similar wage, their standard of living will be worse than before, rather than better. Personally, technological progress does not make them wealthier but poorer. This is why workers in the early capitalist era turned against machines, and to this day there is a belief that the production is the better the more labour it requires.

The stoker on the electric train

Sometimes trade unions or states have engaged in attempts to artificially preserve technologically obsolete activities with the aim of saving jobs. The classic example is the stoker who was still aboard British trains even after the replacement of steam locomotives with electric engines. Prime Minister Margaret Thatcher put an end to this after defeating the trade unions. In technological terms she was right, yet in social terms it was a brutal decision, since the former stokers would basically never have another opportunity to find a new job with decent pay.

Based on a well-justified distrust of capitalism's approach to labour-saving technology, the digital revolution tends to be perceived primarily as a threat to our wealth rather than an opportunity. Two scientists from Oxford University recently created a stir with a study arguing that by 2033, 47 percent of all jobs in the United States would be obsolete as a result of automatization and computerization.[80] While their prediction may be exaggerated, the trend they describe is real.

It is predictable that self-driving cars will at some point replace the taxi industry, and urban trains and buses will no longer need drivers, either. Some people may well miss the chatty cab driver, and we will not necessarily feel safer on local transport without the presence of personnel. But perhaps we will get used to it. It is also quite probable that parcel delivery service will be taken over by small drones, while in supermarkets we will simply pass through electronic gates where all our shopping is scanned automatically, telling us what we owe. If the former cashiers, couriers, taxi drivers, and bus drivers are re-trained and find a job somewhere else with a similar wage, they will probably not be missing their old work. Who does not want to spend their time engaged in more creative and demanding work?

The prospect of an increase in productivity resulting from dig-italization could be a positive thing since it might free our lives from hard work and stress, while opening up new spaces for in-teresting kinds of work. But the problem is that in the context of existing economic and political power structures, this will not be the outcome. As long as the highest possible return rather than a good life is the measure of our economic activities, the replacement of labour by capital on a large scale will serve primarily to destroy livelihoods while further shifting power to capital owners. If former postal workers and taxi drivers, just like miners and steel workers before them, become hopeless long-term unemployed who cannot find other jobs, then digital technologies will make societies poorer rather than richer. It is thus the structure of the capitalist economy itself that keeps us from using technological progress for everyone's well-being.

Technologies that make you sick

There is a further problem. Earlier, we referred to the incentive to adopt labour-saving innovations as the *innovation engine* of capi-talism. But this incentive has no specific direction. Almost any la-bour-saving innovation that lowers production costs is worthwhile for the entrepreneur. Yet quite a few of these innovations are anything but a step forward.

For example, agricultural yields per worker can be pushed up by the extensive use of artificial fertilizers and pesticides, and in animals by the use of growth hormones and antibiotics. The smaller and more horrific the cages for chickens, the more eggs the facility will produce at practically the same level of work. Organic vegetables, at least those that are actually produced by organic farmers, are more expensive than industrially produced vegetables, since they require a much greater input of labour. Thus there are forms of saving labour that do not make a society richer but sicker, yet that nevertheless have a payoff, which is why economic lobbies try their best to prevent or undercut effective laws for consumer and environmental protection. Many production methods in industry requiring little labour come home to roost in the form of creeping environmental destruction, a short shelf life, or limited recyclability.

In addition, there are types of work we might not ever wish to be done by robots. From the viewpoint of capital exploitation, it appears as a major drawback that many areas of the service sector are so far not very capital-intensive and therefore not very suitable for capitalist production. Monopoly positions, such as in private hospitals or digital services, ensure high profits, but in many service sector industries, the market still functions while there is no room for productivity gains, automatization, or economies of scale. A haircut takes the same time today as it did 100 years ago, and the time required to teach a child basic literacy is also much the same.

Digitalization appears to open up new opportunities in these sectors. No doubt online services may be a helpful supplement to regular instruction and study. But no one should wish for an educational system in which online courses and tests replace a large portion of teachers and university professors. Very few people are able to acquire knowledge on their own and without any exchange. Nonetheless, this is a project that some actors in the digital economy are seriously pursuing. And if states under the neoliberal regime continue to lose revenue, the idea to make up for teacher shortages through online courses will before long find advocates in German and European politics. The predictable result will be a further decline in the educational system, further magnifying the differences between children with parental support and those without.

Cared for by robots

The vision of an instructor-free education system is topped by another idea from the digital chamber of horrors—cut-price care homes with a minimal staff, where fully automatized robots wash the elderly and supply their food and beverages. In certain areas today this is technologically feasible, and robots are in fact being employed in senior care—for washing, lifting, and even physical affection. This is in line with a dominant trend. Care work is cut into calculable portions so it could also be carried out by robots: minor clean-up, major clean-up, feeding support ... What old people need at least as much as food and cleaning are affection and human closeness. There is already too little time for this today, and it would eventually be gone completely.

A sombre idea, but one that would make economic sense and that would therefore fit well into our deeply commercialized society. Wealthy seniors will of course continue to be able to afford homes where they are cared for by people. However, public insurance systems could save considerable amounts of money if robot care homes were introduced for the less well-heeled clientele. It is therefore quite easy to predict that unless current social priorities and power realities change, this is what the future will look like.

Top-of-the-line cars and happy children

In an economy that makes sense, the application of labour-saving technologies in sectors where they can be used constructively should create space to focus our work on other areas—such as health care, daycare for children, or even schools and universities. But this can be done only if the profits from growing productivity do not exclusively benefit those industries where the profits are made. Why is it more important for us nowadays to manufacture top-of-the-line cars than to ensure quality early childhood education and exemplary senior care? Because top-of-the-line cars can turn a high profit from which employees for the most part benefit as well. Wages for activities, on the other hand, that no robot can (or should) make more profitable, are often appallingly low—for the educator playing with our children, the primary school teacher from whom they receive their first formal education, or the caregiver who helps our sick or elderly relatives.

In a society in which status and respect are essentially defined through money, it means that those who build cars or maintain machines enjoy a higher social standing than someone earning their money by lovingly caring for other people. As long as this doesn't change, we should not be surprised that a great deal more social creativity will be focused on the question of how to improve the performance and design of our sports cars than on how to make possible a beautiful childhood for kids and a dignified old age for seniors. The question is: is this what we want? Are those really our priorities? We should not let this question be decided for us by the commercial sector.

De-professionalization: idiots instead of skilled workers

Even in the manufacturing sector not every unit of labour saved represents progress. The profit motive is also a strong incentive to favour technologies that de-professionalize work. The work of craftspeople, which requires specific skills, or other forms of qualified skilled labour, are being replaced as much as possible by activities that require barely any qualifications. This too may make economic sense, since unskilled labour can be had more cheaply. As long as the price of labour, like that of potatoes or cars, is determined by the market, it will be proportionately lower the more competition there is for a particular job. And for simple jobs that in principle anybody could do, competition will be much greater than for jobs requiring special skills and training.

In a growing number of sectors, capitalism has replaced crafts-based quality production with industrial mass production, thus devaluing existing knowledge and skills. In many sectors this could be done without a loss in quality and can be a step forward. The spinning jenny, the first industrial spinning machine, devalued the laboriously acquired artisanal skill of weavers overnight. Nevertheless, no one would argue humankind would have done better to stick with the spinning wheel. Moreover, new technologies also gave rise to new qualified jobs—engineers did not exist in the past and prior to the digital age there were no computer scientists. However, there are sectors in which mechanization occurs at the price of quality loss, and de-professionalization represents a clear step backwards.

Ikea culture

The cheapest way to produce residential space, for instance, is the high-rise made of standardized concrete slabs, while the cheapest way to furnish a place is to buy cardboard cabinets that you have to put together yourself. Yet most people would probably prefer living in a stylish building with a small number of units, high ceilings and elegant wooden furniture. There will always be times when it is important to build as many flats as quickly as possible because people who are freezing need a roof over their heads. But this applies to emergencies, and only then.

This is the same situation we encountered with the Michelin-starred restaurants. The more we leave what can be standardized to automated devices, the more time society should have to build really nice flats not only for high earners, and to manufacture decent furniture for people with average incomes—in short, to invest more labour where we need well-trained and qualified personnel.

You might respond that people should be able to buy whatever they like. No one is forced to shop at the cheap stores. For every cheap product, there is a premium version available. We are free to have a qualified cabinetmaker construct a custom-made bookshelf for us.

Well, anyone who can afford it. The fact that many people cannot afford it in spite of the productivity gains of the past decades is also a result of a power shift between working people and capital owners that has put downward pressure on wages. Furniture manufacturing, for example, in the past included the assembly of a desk or wardrobe as a matter of course. Nowadays the average consumer receives a box full of individual parts from which, huffing and puffing, you have to build a usable piece of furniture in your spare time. Only for those willing to pay a hefty surcharge or who frequent very expensive stores will this work be included.

Whereas in the past it was normal even for the average earner to purchase furniture, household appliances, etc. fully assembled, nowadays it is a luxury you have to be able to afford. The infamous Ikea culture has shifted part of the labour process from the manufacturer to private households, i.e. from experts to voluntary or less than voluntary do-it-yourselfers. Those who used to do this work professionally no longer have a sought-after qualification and their jobs have been rationalized away.

7.2 A self-reinforcing process

The U.S. Nobel laureate Paul Samuelson has described the effect of globalization on our wealth, i.e. the shift of labour to low-wage countries, as follows: "That we can get certain things 20 percent cheaper does not necessarily outweigh wage losses which have occurred because these things are now manufactured in China."[81] A shift in the location of production does not necessarily make for lower quality products, it just means that the work is done somewhere else. Whether or not quality will decline, those who had jobs in the affected sectors are earning less today or can't find a new job, so the demand for cheap products will in any case go up. It is a self-reinforcing process.

Following the same logic, skilled jobs may be destroyed by new technologies without any new jobs or just low-wage jobs taking their place. Under those conditions as well, it is highly probable that quality will decline. If such developments are occurring in a number of industries at the same time, ultimately the income losses resulting from a devaluation of skills and professional qualifications will ensure that there will be a demand for new cheap products. The more skilled workers lose their job and the greater the number of well-paid jobs lost, the greater the problem for the remaining high quality producers to sell their products. In the end this is not only a way of destroying individual wealth. An economy's capacity to produce high-value products will also decline. As a result, things that in the past many people were able to afford are once again becoming a luxury for the few.

Nightmares from Silicon Valley

Saving labour is thus not everywhere a desirable goal. Particularly in the case of skilled labour, we should take a closer look at the implications before applauding an innovation that purports to replace such labour with an automated device. This is especially true for the apocalyptic horror scenarios that Silicon Valley is trying to sell to us as a desirable future. Ultimately, they boil down to the end of qualified labour.

In future, according to this upbeat message, everybody will be able to do everything because no one can do anything properly anymore, since no one gets paid for their abilities. The only qualifications that remain will be the software and algorithms analyzing the endless stream of big data and making our decisions for us.

Who needs a banking consultant if the algorithm knows so much more about us and, like divine judgment in its inscrutable ways, is able to determine whether we are creditworthy or not. Who needs journalism if the algorithm extracts from millions of news items those with the most clicks, presenting them to us in an attractive and organized fashion. But, one might object, someone has to write these news articles and put them online. No problem, there are enough people who put things on the Internet, they just shouldn't expect to be paid for it. Who needs a *Michelin Guide* when the Internet is full of user reviews, and anyone who has made an online restaurant reservation through a digital provider will not be left alone until they have submitted their review. Who needs encyclopaedias in the age of *Wikipedia* with its large number of unpaid contributors? And why should health insurance pay for consultations with professional physicians in case of minor problems when we have so many health blogs on the Internet where you can do a search for your little aches and pains and receive from the net community many well-intentioned suggestions for their treatment?

Don't get me wrong: This is not to dismiss the often highly qualified contributions people post online without asking for any compensation whatsoever. This is not to deny that Wikipedia is an excellent aid for many questions and can be much more up-to-date than any encyclopaedia published in book form. There are highly informative blogs that are written for free. And it should not be denied that restaurant or hotel reviews by guests may be helpful in avoiding a disappointing night out or a spoiled vacation. The point is that such services cannot replace professional ones. And if the latter are no longer able to finance themselves, they will disappear. To be sure, rather than progress this would be a huge loss.

Inflatable children's toys

The potential of 3-D printers is at the centre of the debate about the future of professional skills. The most audacious advocates of the digital economy believe that, in future, the manufacturing of the whole spectrum of consumer goods will shift to our homes. Owning such a printer and the corresponding software will enable everyone to construct and produce their own individual house, car, and sofa according to their personal preferences.

As a matter of fact, such printers are already being used in certain areas, and it does appear that they actually will contribute to individualizing automatic production by taking into account specific customer preferences. Of course it is a far-fetched idea that products such as cars, which are developed and constructed based on highly specialized knowledge and skilled labour, in the future will be magically created by do-it-yourselfers. What is not so far-fetched, however, is that even in this sector super cheap products may indeed crowd out quality work. It may well be that one day such printers will indeed spit out drivable boxes that look like inflatable children's toys. If one day such monsters do populate our streets in large numbers, while an elegant automobile with genuine high technology and the latest safety features has become a rare sight, we can be sure of one thing: The reason will not be that a majority of people all of a sudden find the Google car more attractive and more comfortable than an Audi or a BMW.

3-D printing visions

There are areas where 3-D printing makes sense and where production will undoubtedly increase, whereas there are other digital horror visions that would ultimately imply an application of the Ikea model to all areas of life. Why should a surgeon with the ability to do excellent knee surgery have to program some printer to deliver her consumer goods? This is as absurd as expecting a Ph.D. candidate who is working on a new mathematical proof that she herself should put together the shelves for her personal library of specialized books. Division of labour, specialization, and professionalization have been the foundation for humanity's growing wealth over past centuries. The levelling of professional skills would certainly not extend our freedom and quality of life, but would be a step back.

It should give pause to the advocates of an unconditional basic income that their concept originates in the same school of thought. If skills no longer count and special abilities and qualifications no longer result in monetary compensation, you will still have to survive somehow. But such a future is not inevitable, and we should do what we can to prevent it from happening.

Lost self-respect

If such visions were pure fantasy, we could simply ignore them. Unfortunately, they describe a real trend. The de-professionalization of the U.S. economy is far advanced. Aside from the digital economy and the financial industry, the only other sector currently still booming is the weapons industry. Europe is not quite as far advanced yet—the discussion in Germany is still about a lack of skilled workers. But we shouldn't deceive ourselves. Contrary to what this discussion suggests, in Germany there are currently more than 2 million skilled workers as well as 280,000 individuals with postsecondary education who work in what is called a "mini-job" (a monthly wage below 450 euros)—which is to say, they are de facto unemployed. And this is the case despite the fact that the education system makes sure that only a very small number of new skilled workers are trained. In other European countries the situation is even worse. It is therefore not improbable that the future scenarios of Silicon Valley will be coming true since they are consistent with the trends in today's financial and information capitalism.

The idea of an economy in which most people will not have any specific qualifications does not only imply that we would be losing a great deal of our wealth. What is much worse is that individuals in such an environment would be deprived of an essential part of their self-respect. Aristotle already knew that people do not just want to have their basic needs satisfied, but that they want to use their innate or acquired talents, and that they will be the more satisfied with their work the more challenging or complicated it is.

It is because humans are humans that we want to be not only well-fed but also recognized. The more sophisticated an activity and the fewer other people are capable of doing it, the greater as a rule will be the recognition for it. This is why the obsolescence of stupid, boring and unchallenging jobs as a result of digitalization is a step forward rather than a catastrophe. However, precisely because there will be fewer and fewer unqualified jobs, it will be all the more important to allow each of us to develop our own talents through education and training so that we will become capable of doing some thing particularly well and in a professional manner.

Rare losers

Incidentally, there is empirical proof that virtually anyone with a good education is capable of good performance in a particular field. The proof lies in the fact that most children of wealthy parents make it. Unless you want to go out on a limb by arguing that parental wealth is an indicator of the children's particular intelligence, you have to admit that the graduates of expensive private schools are randomly selected—they are those children that happen to have been born into a wealthy family. Of course occasionally you find among them complete failures, but they are remarkably rare. Especially in light of the fact that someone who can look forward to an inheritance of tens or hundreds of millions is clearly less motivated for high achievement than a young person whose future wealth will depend exclusively on her own performance. Thus we can assume that with top education for all, the number of failures will be even lower than among the graduates of the most expensive private schools and boarding schools.

Clearly there are limitations to what education can do. Einstein would probably not have made a good tenor and Luciano Pavarotti perhaps might have made a poor computer scientist. It is also doubtful that the autistic mathematician and game theorist John Forbes Nash would have made a good director of romantic movies. The question is not whether anybody might be capable of anything given a good education, but rather that virtually everybody has some talent that would make them capable of above-average performance in a particular field.

Such a perspective should get us quite a bit closer to a good life than the proposal to lead a nondescript existence as an eternal dilettante sustained by a basic income. A basic income admittedly would be preferable to the tribulations of a Hartz IV welfare recipient or the daily humiliations of many low-wage jobs today, but as an ideal it is completely inadequate. This conception would only be convincing if the assumption was correct that a considerable part of humanity cannot be educated and is not capable of professional work. This is not only an unattractive view of humanity, it is also and above all false.

A good life is therefore not a matter of abstract growth figures. Not GDP, size of the capital stock, monetary assets, or even productivity are ultimate measures for a society's prosperity. In general terms we might say the following. Technologies replacing monotonous, boring and repetitive work tend to make us richer, since the less time a society needs to spend on supplying goods for the satisfaction of basic needs, the more time it has for other things. However, the more modern technologies free us from monotonous and boring activities, the more professional qualification and specialization we need. This, at any rate, would be the progressive counter-proposal to the idea of excluding the majority of people from the opportunity to achieve recognition and respect in a particular job, goading them with the prospect that they will be able to contribute their two cents on the Internet on whatever matter they want.

And what if some day technology will reduce the necessary volume of professional work as well? All the better. Who says that we should pursue our profession eight hours a day forever? If four or five hours are sufficient to provide what we need for a good life—

great. Then we'll finally have more time for all those other things that in addition to meaningful work are indispensable for a happy life—for our loved ones and our friends, for reading good books or going to beautiful concerts, for jogging, bicycling, playing soccer, or simply lying in the sun listening to birdsong and the humming of the bumble bees.

8. ANOTHER WAY IS POSSIBLE: COOPERATIVE BANKS

8.1 Master or servant:
What kind of financial industry do we need?

The images travelled around the world. In the early summer of 2015, long lines formed in front of cash machines and banks in Greece. A desperate pensioner complains on camera that he's not able to buy the medication his wife needs because there is no access to cash. The Greek economy is on the brink of collapse. How lucky we are, some may have thought—and some journalists in fact wrote—that in 2008 we saved our banks across Europe. While that was very costly and drove up the public debt, it spared us from seeing similar images in Berlin and Paris.

In fact, the banking crisis of 2008/2009 and the crisis in Greece in the summer of 2015 were caused by completely different factors. Seven years earlier, the banks stumbled because they had gorged themselves on high risk papers and bad loans. When the debtors—U.S. house owners and Spanish real estate speculators—were no longer able to service their loans, causing massive losses in the derivatives based on these loans, losses piled up that far exceeded the capital of financial institutions. In order to prevent them from going bankrupt, states took over a large part of these losses. Public funds in excess of 4,500 billion (or 4.5 trillion) dollars were made available for this purpose in Europe alone. Bad loans of around 1,000 billion are still on the balance sheets of European banks. However, since the European Central Bank is flooding financial markets with cheap money, creating a state of permanent euphoria, few really care—until they are rudely awakened by the next crash.

Paper euros

In 2015 Greek banks sat on top of a mountain of bad debt—no big surprise after five years of economic depression that had already destroyed one quarter of Greece's economic performance. But the trigger for those dramatic scenes was a different one. Greece was running short on cash. The sudden spike in demand was accounted for by fears on the part of the Greek population that their accounts might be switched back to the old currency, the drachma, in the process losing a substantial part of their value. This could not happen to a paper euro. For this reason the Greek population would have preferred to exchange their entire electronic euro holdings, i. e. the money in their checking accounts, into paper euros. An unusual situation since normally we consider the two kinds of euros to be equivalent. After all, with your bank card and electronic money you can pay for the same things that you buy with cash—unless the receiver is trying to evade taxes. The card has the additional advantage of having a PIN number, while cash money is lost when it is stolen.

For this reason, cash money usually no longer plays a central role in our lives. We pay for more than 80 percent of our purchases electronically. The situation was quite different in Greece in June 2015. After influential European politicians such as German finance minister Wolfgang Schäuble had publicly speculated about a return to the drachma, the Greeks worried about a devaluation of their money. This prospect unsettled them more than the fear of being robbed. In other words, they wanted cash. Cash itself is only paper banknotes, the supply of which can be easily increased. The problem, however, is that while banks are authorized to issue electronic money (and almost without limitations, as we will see), they are not permitted to print banknotes. Since the introduction of the euro, the Greek Central Bank has not been permitted to do so; printing money is exclusively done by the European Central Bank. Its job is to ensure the cash supply in the euro area. Well, at least in principle.

As the events in Greece have demonstrated, supplying the economy and the population with money is not simply a technical problem but an intensely political issue. In the early summer of 2015 the unruly Greek leftist government wanted to put an end to the policy of cutbacks dictated by the so-called troika of European Central Bank, International Monetary Fund, and European Commission. The Greek government had held a referendum on this question and won over 60 percent of the vote. There were obvious political interests in favour of forcing the Greek government to back down. Germany, Spain, as well as many Eastern European governments were among those interested parties. But the European Central Bank, which for the first time exerted its power without any restraint, made the decisive move. In spite of a growing demand for money, the bank restricted the supply of euro banknotes, further strengthening the desire for paper instead of electronic euros. As a result, with monetary transfers coming to an almost complete halt, the Greek economy was on the brink of collapse.

The blackmail worked, the Greek Syriza government caved in. As soon as the new program of cutbacks, which in its brutality far exceeded previous ones, was signed, the ECB resumed its job. People could again withdraw as much cash as they wanted. Gradually, the demand for cash subsided as speculation about a reintroduction of the drachma—at least for the time being—died down.

Key industry financial economy

The fact that the Greek problems of early summer 2015 have been confused with the question of saving the banks at the start of the most recent major financial crisis clearly indicates just how little the working of our current financial system is understood. How does money come into existence today? Who launches it into circulation? Why does today's financial system obviously not work the way it should? And why have the periods between financial crises over the past 30 years become shorter and shorter while their extent has grown dramatically?

No one can deny that the financial sector is of central importance for the development of an economy. All decisions that determine future prosperity—on research, investment, innovation, and the promotion of ideas—are related not only to entrepreneurial considerations but above all to the availability of funds. It would be the task of a well-functioning financial sector to allocate funds to economic sectors that can create a rising standard of living by using better, i. e. labour-saving and sustainable, technologies.

Loans or other types of financing are in demand from a wide range of enterprises—from corporations to small producers, from innovative start-ups to self-satisfied monopolists, from hostile takeover projects to speculative hedge funds. It is up to the banks to decide whose requests will be fulfilled and who will lose in the competitive race for money. This represents incredible power. You might think that a society has a strong interest in making sure that such power is used responsibly and does not fall into the wrong hands. Seen in this light, it is baffling how long and with what equanimity we have tolerated the fact that the key industry "financial economy" is profoundly and permanently damaging our prosperity on a global scale.

Köhler's monster

In the spring of 2008, the president of the Federal Republic of Germany, Horst Köhler, compared the international financial industry with a monster that was increasingly losing touch with the real economy. In the fall of the same year, it became abundantly clear what he had in mind, when the U.S. investment bank Lehman Brothers collapsed, taking down with it a large number of big and small banks, insurance companies, and other financial institutions around the world. More accurately, this is what would have happened had states not saved them at the cost of a rapidly increasing public debt.

Suddenly issues previously known only to experts on the international financial system became the subject of public debate: the obscure methods that for many years allowed large investment banks to earn absurd sums of money; the extent to which non-transparent financial instruments were dumped on the market—derivatives that in 2003 U.S. investor Warren Buffett called "financial weapons of mass destruction"; and the extent to which manipulation, explicit and implicit fraud, and other criminal machinations were part of the business model.

This realization produced a general feeling of shock, sanctimonious commitments from governments to root out the dangers of financial speculation, as well as one or the other half-hearted regulatory initiative that, if not immediately defanged by the financial lobby, just disappeared in the archives. The bankers were biding their time until the storm blew over, then returned to their desks and computers to continue working in the same way as before. Yet the stakes of the game they were playing had only increased as a result of the crisis.

State liability

We continue to tolerate the arrogant gamblers in the sales offices of the large betting shops we still call banks, and not only that—we even finance them. It was thanks to the many billions of dollars and euros that after a brief phase of uncertainty everything could continue as if there had never been a crash. Martin Hellwig, former Chair of the German Monopoly Commission and now a conservative critic of the banks, writes: "It is as if we were subsidizing the chemical industry so that they pollute our rivers and lakes, thus encouraging them to produce more pollution."[82] The situation is indeed pretty insane.

In Europe the project of a European banking union was launched, which for the first time established by law what previously had been only a de facto state liability guarantee for private banks. It was celebrated as major progress that in future, owners and creditors were to participate in the financial rehabilitation of a failed bank. *Participate!* That is, up to a maximum of 8 percent of the bank's debt.

This fact alone demonstrates how far public debate has moved away from any market principles when dealing with banks. Why are its owners merely "participating" when a private enterprise goes bankrupt? In what other industry is their share of liability limited to 8 percent of the debt? In case of bankruptcy in the regular economy, owners lose their shares. If it is a partnership, even the owners' private assets are included in the bankruptcy assets.

We permit the banks, on the other hand, to continue engaging in transactions of trillions of dollars with minimal equity of their own. While a medium-sized engineering company with less than 20 percent equity is not considered creditworthy, the large banks operate with equity capital of about 3 percent. And then European legislation is passed guaranteeing that not even those 3 percent will be included in case of bankruptcy, but only a portion thereof, and only to the extent that it won't threaten the institution's financial stability. A scene from the insane asylum, it seems. But this has become the reality we live in.

"They have made their own rules ..."

Of course state failure is the other side of the power that we have given the financial industry, which feeds on itself, becoming ever larger and more powerful. Jamie Dimon, Chair of the Board of JPMorgan Chase, which during the financial crisis rose to the rank of largest U.S. bank as a result of concluding very advantageous mergers, once remarked that his financial institution made a "good return in the bank's 'seventh business segment'—relations to the political establishment and the state bureaucracy."[83] And Joseph Stiglitz, Nobel laureate in economics, responded to the question why Goldman Sachs emerged as a winner from both the Asian financial crisis of 1997 and the financial crisis of 2008 as follows: "They have co-written the rules which permit them to do exceedingly well even in crises they have caused themselves."[84]

The monster was set free during the global deregulation of financial markets in the early 1980s. From then on there was no stopping it. Whereas in the late 1970s, 100 billion dollars a day were traded on global currency markets, it is now over 4,000 billion. The annual volume of financial derivatives was less than 50 trillion dollars, the global casino is now trading 1,500 trillion derivatives every year. In the twenty years between 1990 and 2010 in which the size of the world economy tripled, the financial economy expanded by a factor of 300. The balance sheet of Deutsche Bank today is forty times that of its 1980 value.

Money incest

Only 2 percent of global financial transactions have any relationship with the real economy. The financial gamblers prefer to trade with their own, i. e. with banks or other financial service institutions. An example for such incestuous monetary transactions is high frequency trade, which by now accounts for 70–80 percent of business in U.S. stock exchanges. In terms of the real economy, such transactions make no sense at all, much like most derivatives and bills. However, the manipulation of market prices generates billions in risk-free revenue for the financial institutions.

There is probably no other economic sector in which so much money is earned without providing any relevant product. This is possible since the economic power and closed markets in the case of oligopolies we discussed earlier apply to the financial sector as well. The global financial market is essentially run by the insider deals of a handful of large banks and a few large capital fund managers. Their "put" or "call" determines the value of currencies, bonds, and shares just as much as it does the interest rates a state pays on public debt.

Masters of the universe

That investment bankers should think themselves masters of the universe was occasionally ridiculed or viewed as a sign of their hubris during the financial crisis. But actually they are not suffering from an exaggerated sense of self-importance—they are indeed the masters of our economy because we have made so. So-called financial experts of the kind frequently invited to talk shows tell us that the "judgment of the markets" should be accepted not only by firms but by states as well. If "the markets" are of the opinion that Spain should pay 10 percent for its government bonds, this is viewed as the judgment by a sacred source, which humans ought not question. But who are "the markets"? For the emission of European government bonds, there are about 15 large international banks that are authorized by states with the exclusive right to place government bonds. This is not just a closed market, it is no market at all. It is 15 self-assured investment bankers whom we have given the right to make decisions on our prosperity and the financial room for manoeuvre of elected governments.

There is no need to discuss the quality of these "market judgments", since prior to 2010 Greece received loans far exceeding the acceptable limits of public debt. More important, such a distribution of power between private institutions and elected governments makes democracy simply impossible. In this context it is not surprising that all attempts at government regulation have failed. Those who control the flow of money hold the longer end of the stick.

For this reason there is no such thing as the soft regulation of the financial industry. Either you cut the base of their power—their virtually limitless ability to generate money, which they use to make incredible profits and channel into economically unproductive or even destructive activities—or you lose. "Give me control over a nation's money, and I won't care who makes the laws," the legendary founder of the Rothschild banking dynasty, Mayer Amschel Rothschild, observed at the end of the eighteenth century. Without a change in monetary order there cannot be a different economic order.

Small and stable

There was a time when bankers had few friends among politicians and even among economists. After the stock market crash on Wall Street and other financial centres had led the world economy into many years of depression with millions unemployed and dramatic political consequences, some lessons were learned. The financial institutions were put into a tight corset and virtually everything was regulated—interest on savings and loans, admissible fields of activity for commercial banks, de facto even the quantity of loans they were permitted to issue. The banks where your average Joe had an account and which gave loans to normal firms were small and stable. The radius of their commercial activities was regional, or at most national, and they were not engaged in trading shares. The job of a banker was boring, secure, and moderately paid—more suitable to honest employees with a public servant mentality than for high-flying minds with special mathematical talents. Stock markets were a place for trading shares and bonds, but without untransparent securities, and the volume of trade was low.

It was clearly a better financial system. In the period between 1945 and 1971 there were no significant banking crises. No one missed all the derivatives, securitizations, and other financial innovations, which the financial lobby now—wrongly—tells us are of fundamental economic significance.

That a small financial sector is more beneficial for the real economy than a bloated one pursuing its own incestuous money transactions and bets on derivatives can by now be considered a well-established fact. Numerous studies have confirmed that firms in countries with a large financial sector have reduced access to investment and innovation funds, which is why there is a negative relationship between the size of a country's financial sector and its economic growth.[85] Why this is the case can be easily understood. The financial industry should have the task of channelling funds into economic investments that make all of us more prosperous. If instead its primary activity is directing money into channels that only make financial gamblers richer, then the economy will necessarily have a lower level of development.

High-flying investment bankers

This has also been the German experience. When, around the turn of the millennium, Deutsche Bank, the other large private banks, as well as state banks started to do "investment banking on the high bar", as Deutsche Bank's former Chairman of the Board, Rolf-E. Breuer, referred to the bank's new goal, lending by those banks collapsed almost completely. Had Germany not had the savings banks and credit unions, which were partially able to make up for this decline, medium-sized businesses, usually celebrated as "the backbone of our economy", would have rapidly declined.

In conventional textbooks, banks are often represented as so-called intermediaries between savers and investors. Collecting individuals' savings, they pass on the capital to those who are willing to go into debt. A criticism of the banks with respect to this model would be that they direct savings into the wrong channels. This would be bad enough, but reality is even worse. If the banks were only money brokers, they would never have become this powerful. The banks in our time don't distribute money, they create it, and almost without limit. The money they have created is then channelled for the most part into the financial economy rather than the real economy. Why bother with small borrowers if it is so much easier and vastly more profitable to earn money in financial commerce? In this way, today's financial industry feeds itself, becoming larger and more powerful, while—especially smaller—enterprises willing to invest are left to starve.

8.2 Where does money come from?

In order to better understand how the financial industry works, the following section will discuss the question what money is and how it Is made, looking at both past and present. Unfortunately, a certain degree of abstraction is unavoidable. If you have no interest in these more theoretical questions, you are advised to skip this section and continue reading the following section entitled "Money is a public good". This is also where a proposal for a new monetary order is developed.

Speaking about money, many people may still be thinking about gold or silver coins, even though none of us has personal experience of such currencies. Money is related to gold only if gold is given a monetary function. What are the functions of money? First, and this has also been historically its original function, money is a unit of accounting with which goods and services are valued, which makes it possible to balance accounts.

To the extent that we are dealing with manufactured goods, it stands to reason that the value of a good is related to the work that has gone into its production. If the production of one kilogram of wheat requires twice as much work, or the employment of twice as many slaves, as the production of one kilogram of oats, this suggests that one kilogram of wheat is given double the value.

Bookkeeping of debts and assets

Bookkeeping of debts and assets is almost as old as economic activity itself. The reason is simple. Economic production requires time, and in order to bridge this time, the producer needs either to have reserves or someone who will let you pay up later. The latter generates debt that has to be measured in a certain *unit*. Those, on the other hand, who first supply goods without receiving immediate compensation, are building up claims or assets. Bookkeeping of debts and assets can be done in cuneiform writing on stone or scoring tallies on willow trees—how it is done doesn't matter.

The usefulness of such a credit system is evident. It lends the creditor purchasing power she would not otherwise have. Without the opportunity to go into debt, her reserves would constitute the limit for planning purposes. Lean periods as a result of poor harvests or other calamities could thus be bridged without immediately starving to death. There has never been an economy without debt, and as such debt is not a bad thing, on the contrary: it makes possible economic projects that otherwise would not happen.

However, the downside of the debt system was already known in early antiquity—excessive indebtedness. Interest can drive up debt quickly, especially if the debtor is using it primarily for consumption rather than profitable investment. In order to prevent a majority of the population from falling into debt bondage and becoming serfs, ancient communities would from time to time cancel all debts.

A special kind of debt that also emerged early is debts from taxes that states impose on their subjects. Already the old Sumerians financed their state through levies that were calculated with the measuring unit they called the *shekel*.

Symbols as means of payment

To start with, money is merely a unit of calculation in order to make debt possible and thus create additional purchasing power. Debt measures the value of goods, work, or taxes in a common unit of accounting. We refer to this unit as a *currency*. It may be called shekel, guilder, euro, or whatever.

Obviously this is not the only function of money. We don't just incur debt or build up assets, but we *pay* with money. When we have bought and paid for cherries at the grocer's, we don't owe him any-thing, he has our money, we're all paid up. Since the seventh centu-ry before the start of the Christian calendar, when the first evidence for the existence of coins is available, money has not only been a measuring unit for calculating debts and assets, but also a *means of payment*.

In order to use it as such, we need some thing that represents a certain number of measuring units and that we can give to the seller. It is better if this thing is not too large or heavy. Some peo-ple used cows as a means of payment, but this is not very practical. Bars of precious metal were also used very early as payment. But this too is cumbersome. For small amounts, extremely accurate scales are needed, and for large purchases you would have to carry heavy weights. This is why it has become standard to just pay with sym-bols, the material value of which is significantly lower than the value of the goods that could be purchased with it.

The most important condition for being able to pay with a sym-bol is of course that the seller is willing to let us have her goods in exchange for this symbol. Symbols useful for this purpose are small round pieces of metal, paper notes, or digital entries on hard drives. They give us purchasing power if our counterpart accepts them.

Paper money from the colour printer

A woman we shall call Ellie Rich might use her colour printer to pro-duce small colourful bills with flowers and numbers. She could call her currency the *ellar*. If she finds a group of people who agree to value garden crops and mutual services in ellars and to accept these bills, then Ellie will be able to lend her bills to someone who pur-chases zucchini and potatoes from the garden of another person, so he can make it to his next salary payment. He then goes to fix a bro-ken water pipe for the vegetable grocer, receiving in turn Ellie's bills, which he returns to her, adding a few strawberries by way of interest.

Alternatively, Ellie herself may go shopping with her bills and have the cherry harvest from all others delivered to her.

Ellie's problem is that it might be difficult to find people who sell cherries, zucchini or potatoes in exchange for ellar bills, and even more difficult to find someone willing to borrow them. After all, anybody could print bills with flowers and numbers saying "5 ellars" or "10 ellars". They would fulfill the same purpose without the need to go into debt. But those bills will hardly serve as money. It is not because it costs little to produce them, but because there is no reason why others should accept them.

True, there are exchange networks working along these lines. However, their currencies tend to be exclusively units of calculation, based on the agreement that hours of work or other services are accounted for in this currency. For good reason no one is authorized to print this currency, since they would be in the privileged position of receiving the services of others without giving anything in return simply by printing bills. Moreover, with this kind of incentive there would probably soon be more bills in circulation than members of the network who would be willing and able to babysit or do work in the garden. Exchange circles with their own currencies may survive for extended periods, but usually just on a small scale. They work best if members know each other personally. And people will probably be careful not to accumulate claims in this currency above a certain limit because you never know whether they will still be honoured in a few years time.

Another currency that was privately created is the bitcoin. They can be used to do transactions on the Internet. However, not every seller accepts bitcoins as payment. And members of this system have learned that it is not advisable to accumulate large amounts of bitcoins. This is because their value in terms of other currencies, and thus their real purchasing power, is subject to extreme fluctuations.

Government money

The money states put into circulation and accept for the payment of taxes is as a rule generally accepted within the borders of this state. A seller is assured that there is at least one address where these symbols of value will be honoured, i. e. by the state. In Europe state money initially consisted of coins denominated in a certain currency. The coins were made of metal, with the value of the metal usually lower than the value imprinted on the coins.

Money as a unit of value thus permits us to incur debt and in this way to have additional purchasing power. Money as a means of payment provides its owner with a symbol that gives him purchasing power without having to go into debt. It relieves the seller from the risk of his buyer in the end not being able to pay. It is of course always easier to buy than to borrow, and a shortage in the means of payment can seriously harm a country's economic activity. This is precisely what occurred in Greece in the summer of 2015. The section of the population without credit or debit cards—a significant number among older Greeks—were all of a sudden unable to buy anything even though they had money in the bank.

Bonds as a means of payment

After the invention of coins as money, other means of payment emerged as well. Coins were simply not available in sufficient quantities. In addition, long-distance trade was difficult to finance with a means of payment that was accepted only in certain territories. In order to avoid having to transport significant amounts of precious metal, economic actors proved extremely ingenious by introducing symbols into circulation that could be used as means of payment. Bonds, for example, fulfilled this purpose well if debtors were wealthy and respected, making it highly unlikely that upon completion they would not pay their debts.

If, for instance, a Florentine painter in the early sixteenth century was commissioned to produce a portrait of a member of the Medici family, for which he received in advance a document promising him 100 gold coins upon conclusion of the work, chances were good that he would be able to use this paper as a means of payment. He could pass it on to an inn in return for a hot meal a day for a year. The inn could have probably paid a supplier with this promissory note. Commercial bills of well-established businesses were also circulating as means of payment. If a debtor unexpectedly went bankrupt while having numerous bills in circulation, this could strongly affect economic life.

In classical Athens and again after the fourteenth century, deposit banks existed issuing their own bonds that could be used for payment purposes. Basically, these banks did what Ellie Rich would have liked to do—print notes to give them to merchants and other traders who would thus increase their purchasing power for other business projects. Unlike the case of Ellie, the system worked because these notes were generally accepted. The trick consisted in the banks as creditors guaranteeing that they would on request provide the value of the figure on the note in the form of silver or gold. They disposed of precious metal since others were storing their gold and silver in the banks, for which in turn they also received notes they could use as money.

Beheaded bankers

The only precondition for the functioning of this system was the unblemished reputation of the banker. For if customers had actually acted on the promise of receiving precious metals in exchange, the old banks would have met with a similar fate as the Greek banks did in the early summer of 2015. Just as in the latter case, customers held much more electronic money than the bank held in cash, the old bankers had of course printed more notes than there was gold in their vaults. For the bankers concerned, the result would be rather unfortunate. After the bankruptcy of their bank, they would also be personally ruined, living out a their days in debtors' prison. The Catalan authorities even passed a law in 1321, according to which bankers who could no longer honour the claims of their clients would be publicly denounced and beheaded in front of their bank.

In economic terms, this did not make sense, since the gold stored in bank vaults was not directly related to the emitted notes' function as a means of payment. The notes endowed their owner with a specific amount of purchasing power with which to demand goods and services. The notes could fulfill this function completely independently of whether the banks stored tons of gold in their vaults or whether only rats lived there. However, since ultimately the notes were the banks' private bonds, their acceptance was naturally a function of their ability to pay. And in a crisis situation this depended upon their stock of precious metals. This is why the erroneous view emerged that recoverable money had to be secured by silver or gold—a view that has survived for many centuries.

The gold standard

Bank failures in which a significant portion of the means of payment in circulation lost its value would regularly result in economic crises. This is why, in the second part of the nineteenth century, banks in most industrial countries lost their right to print notes. Only the state or a bank specifically invested with a monopoly of producing bank notes, the central bank, would now have this right. From then on not only coins but paper money as well became state money.

That's when the financial architecture emerged that essentially remains in place to this day. It consists of commercial banks that accept deposits and offer loans, maintain accounts, and transfer funds—i. e. increasing the balance of one person and reducing that of another, thus effecting a payment. However, upon request commercial banks have to pay out a deposit in paper money. They therefore have to ensure that their cash holdings are sufficient, since they are not allowed to print any money themselves. The central bank is now responsible for supplying the economy with paper money, which it lends to commercial banks. In addition, the central bank is the lender of last resort, i.e. the emergency credit supplier of banks with the goal of preventing their collapse as a result of liquidity problems.

The currency system that emerged in the nineteenth century differed from our present system in its so-called gold standard. This was based on the theory that the precondition for a stable currency was limiting the quantity of money in circulation to the value of the gold stored in the central bank. For this purpose a fixed value of a currency unit in gold was established, making it possible to exchange a pound sterling or a dollar for a fixed amount of gold at any time.

With brief interruptions, the U.S. dollar was linked to a fixed rate in gold until 1971. However, regular citizens no longer had the option of exchanging their dollars into gold. This right was restricted to other central banks. Theoretically, the U.S. central bank (the "Fed") would have had to cough up one ounce of gold for every 35 dollars. Of course everyone knew that it would not be in a position to do so since, in the three decades following World War II, a much greater amount of dollars was put into circulation than the central bank held in gold. When, on the initiative of President Charles de Gaulle, the French central bank did in fact demand to see gold for its dollars, U.S. President Richard Nixon simply abolished the gold standard.

Deflation and crisis

In the period before World War I and in the 1920s, central banks were quite serious about the gold standard. Rather than trying to keep the money supply of the economy in line with growth and other economic considerations, the primary objective was to protect the fixed exchange rate in gold. On the plus side, there was therefore no inflation in the economy. Instead, shortages in the means of payment and falling prices would occur frequently, with even more damaging consequences for the economy.

Between 1873 and 1879, the price level in Britain declined by 18 percent, and a further 19 percent by 1886. Similarly, from 1870 to 1890 the price index in the United States fell continuously. For consumers this seemed to be a favourable situation, but economically falling prices intensify crises, since deflation means a decline in the value of production but not in the value of debt. As a result, there is an increased danger of over-indebtedness. In such an environment significantly more firms go bankrupt than would be the case with constant or gradually increasing prices.

Fixed exchange rates

An even greater problem was that the gold standard seriously reduced any political room for manoeuvre. Since individual currencies had a fixed relationship to gold, this also fixed their relationship to each other. As a result, at least between the industrialized countries, there were basically no revaluations or devaluations. To this extent, the situation was comparable with what is the case in today's euro area where different states share a common currency. This is why the problems of the past were quite similar to those of today. Already prior to World War I, these countries had close trade relations. In addition, the movement of capital was free and uncontrolled. England, the birthplace of industrialization, continued to be the strongest industrial country in addition to being a large colonial power. The United States and Germany were rapidly catching up. The economic structure of France and other European countries, on the other hand, was still predominantly agrarian.

Whenever countries with different levels and speeds of development trade with each other, this usually results in imbalances. The more productive country will have a trade surplus since its products are more competitive, while the less productive country will have a trade deficit. This will occur if wages in one country stay lower than in another country. The country with lower wages can export more cheaply and therefore export greater quantities while at the same time importing less since lower wages limit consumption. Such a country will therefore realize an export surplus, while other countries are going into debt. What happens is thus precisely what we are familiar with in the euro area today.

If exchange rates are flexible, the currency of surplus countries will appreciate while the currency of deficit countries will depreciate. This means that exports of the more productive or lower-wage country become more expensive while its imports become cheaper. In the end this can re-establish a balance. Under fixed exchange rates or with a common currency, this valve remains closed. It is no accident that since the introduction of the euro, Germany has had 11 consecutive years of balance of payment surpluses of more than 4 percent of GDP, in 8 of those years they were even above 6 percent. Year after year, Germany has thus sold significantly more goods abroad than it has purchased from other countries. Other countries had correspondingly permanent deficits, some running to double figures. As long as currency revaluation and devaluation were possible between European countries, such extreme disparities never existed. Instead, the external value of the deutschmark would increase.

Theoretically, the imbalances under the conditions of the gold standard should have been offset by the movement of gold. The free flow of capital, however, ensured that gold would rarely leave the vaults. Instead of having to pay their deficits in gold, much like today deficit countries received loans.

Gold standard without democracy

All this worked only because at the time everyone assumed that defending fixed exchange rates and gold parity were the supreme goals of every central bank. Responding to large trade deficits thus took the form of interest hikes in order to attract capital. In such a system, individual states have basically lost authority over their currency. They are no longer able to use interest rate policy to target their own economic conditions. Instead, they are forced to respond to imbalances in the international financial balance, even if this means their high interest rate policy will trigger a serious economic crisis at home—with corporate bankruptcies and rapidly increasing unemployment. True, this may lead to a kind of rebalancing of trade, but at a very high price. Deficits have usually gone hand in hand with protectionist measures, i.e. tariff protection of domestic industries. In this way, the exchange rate could be defended.

The U.S. economist Barry Eichengreen argues that the gold standard, with its exchange rates fixed for decades, could be maintained only on account of an absence of democratic structures and the lack of universal and equal voting rights in most industrialized countries. For economic historian Karl Polanyi, the role of the gold standard was above all to enforce policies in the interest of capital owners and at the expense of workers. In order to break the resistance of trade unions and eliminate left parties from government, "currency threats" were repeatedly invoked, while the blame for this was regularly assigned to "inflated wages and budget deficits"[86].

"Currency threats"

Polanyi refers to the brief period during the French popular front government under Leon Blum in the 1930s, which attempted to jump-start the economy using Keynesian policies. The government's scope to create more demand through credit-financed state spending was destroyed by an immediate onset of capital flight. Already in the 1920s, France had experienced that debates about the introduction of a property tax were enough to trigger massive capital flight and a franc currency crisis. As soon as the tax project was abandoned, the external value of the Franc recovered.

Polanyi has strong reasons to believe that without suspending the gold standard, the American New Deal with which U.S. President

Roosevelt fought the economic crisis would have never been possible. "The dethroning of Wall Street [as a result of a timely suspension of the gold standard] in the 1930s saved the United States from a social catastrophe of the continental European kind."[87]

Cashless credit

While the gold standard tied the hands of governments, it did not prevent banks from finding ways and means to expand lending, above all in order to fund financial projects. The central banks' monopoly over paper money was not a problem, since no cash was needed to finance capital transactions.

The stock market bubble of the 1920s, which burst in 1929, was accompanied and inflated by a continuous expansion of bank loans. In order to make stock markets boom, those who buy shares must have additional purchasing power. An indispensable drug for stimulating this purchasing power is the financial credit extended by banks. Of course income distribution also plays a role. A society in which the rich keep earning more and more and normal workers and employees less and less will have a higher demand for shares and a lower demand for mid-range cars. Yet for a genuine bull market this is never enough. What is required is the unlimited growth in the banks' creation of credit, which in turn contributes to making the rich who are active on the stock markets even richer.

In order to close off this channel, one of the consequences of the financial crash of 1929 in the United States and Britain was the institutional separation between credit banks and investment banks. While in Germany there were no such laws, the two central pillars of the German banking sector after 1945 were savings banks and co-operative banks, which as classic credit banks would not get involved in stock market activity. In addition, there were the Deutsche Bank, the Dresdner, and the Commerzbank, all of which owned company shares on a large scale but did not trade them. Most of the other business activities of today's investment banks were simply illegal.

The Bretton Woods system

In the period after World War II, at the international level the gold standard was replaced by the Bretton Woods system. It made the dollar the international reserve currency. U.S. currency thus de facto assumed the role of gold. While formally the dollar itself was tied to gold at a fixed rate, from the start the system worked only because the Fed provided dollars, the international means of payment, in large quantities and far in excess of existing amounts of gold. This was hardly an act of selflessness, since the status of world reserve currency of course came with the great advantage of being able to buy abroad without providing anything in return. Our example of Ellie Rich showed how privileged those with the authority to print a particular currency are. The Fed and the U.S. commercial banks were now "printing" the currency for the whole world. This is why Keynes had suggested that rather than having a national currency elevated into international reserve currency, it would be better to create a fictitious one, the Bancor. For the United States, however, this would have been much less favourable, which is why the Americans rejected Keynes's proposal.

While the exchange rates of all other currencies were fixed with respect to the dollar, they could be changed. The IMF was established in order to grant bridging loans to countries with deficits, while at the same time monitoring their economic policy, thus contributing to a situation in which deficits could be eliminated without altering the exchange rate.

This system however also quickly generated imbalances, i.e. deficits for some countries and surpluses for others. As long as capital flows were strictly regulated, these were caused by imbalances in the real economy. Later, speculative capital movements would further destabilize the Bretton Woods system. It was finally abandoned in 1971 in favour of flexible exchange rates.

Electronic money's march to victory

The first crack in the strict legal regulation of Europe's financial sector appeared in the late 1950s, when Euro markets were being established as an international trading zone for financial transactions. It was of course not euros—which didn't exist at the time—that were traded on Euro markets, but generally foreign currencies that did not fall under the jurisdiction of individual governments. Those governments could have prohibited their banks from engaging in this trade, but for a variety of reasons did not do so.

On Euro markets, but also in the strictly regulated national banking sectors, electronic systems for financial transactions increasingly became the norm. In the early 1960s, wage payments were shifted from cash to direct account deposits. Ever since, digital accounting increasingly marginalized paper money as a means of payment. For banks this was of significant benefit. For electronic money's march to victory meant that banks fully regained their power to create money, which the cash monopoly of central banks had to some extent restricted. In addition, computerization and digitalization were the technological preconditions for the ludicrous business ideas and financial constructs of today's investment banking.

Millions at the click of a mouse

Unlike cash money, private banks have the power to create their own electronic money. This is their great privilege, which is not available to other economic actors. In order to extend loans, banks do not need cash savings or central bank loans. Electronic money is created by a bank representative crediting a checking account. This money thus emerges out of nothing, i.e. simply by the fact that it is being credited.[88]

Let us assume that a generous bank would like to extend a loan of 1 million euros to a valued client by the name of Max Lazybones. As the amount appeared in Max's account, the item "debts of clients" increases the bank's assets by 1 million. How does the bank finance this claim? The bank does its own financing, since with Max's account balance growing by 1 million, the item "liabilities to clients" increases on the liabilities side of the bank's balance sheet. Legally speaking, the money in our account is money we are *lending* to the bank, even if most of us are probably unaware. But this what makes our current monetary system so special.

In terms of its balance sheet, any bank can therefore simply create loans at the click of a mouse. With respect to regulation, the bank only has to ensure that its loans are covered by its own capital at a rate required by law. This rate tends to be rather lax. If the borrower has a good rating, it is possible that for every euro of its own equity, the bank can create 62.5 euros in loans. If the borrower is the state, there are no limits at all. The legal equity requirement is most limiting for the extension of loans to the real economy, in particular small firms and start-ups, which typically do not have a top credit rating. In financial business, on the other hand, innovative financial instruments that are accepted as equity are created at the same time as loans are issued to the real economy.[89] Alternatively, derivatives are used that minimize equity requirements through supposed risk reduction. This is the reason for the economic boom in credit default swaps. With a modicum of imagination and creativity, today's financial institutions active in investment banking have a virtually unlimited ability to create money. In this way they are financing the still unchecked growth of the financial sector as well as constantly growing asset and debt bubbles.

To be fair, it should be mentioned that for certain investments, banks are legally required to maintain a minimum reserve in their account with the central bank. This rule is even less effective in limiting credit extension than the equity rule, since banks can borrow the necessary money from the central bank at any time. All they have to do is pledge any of their infinite number of bonds as collateral.

License to print money

If a business generates risk-free profits on a large scale, we say that someone has a "license to print money". Private banks literally have this license. They are permitted to "print" electronic money on their own and without any authorization. They are not allowed to print paper money. It is therefore of some significance that cash is playing an increasingly minor role, whereas situations as happened in Greece where all of a sudden everybody wants only paper money are the absolute exception.

Let us return to our fortunate Max Lazybones and his 1 million-euro loan. What happens once the amount has been credited to his account? Usually individuals want loans because they have plans of some sort. There is no reason why the money should stay in his account. Let us assume that, true to his name, Max Lazybones treats himself to a luxury vacation in the Maldives, including a first-class flight and a private yacht. He is not going to withdraw the million euros in cash, but will transfer the money to the travel agency where he has booked the trip. If the travel agency has its account with the same bank as he does, nothing changes in the bank's balance sheet. Except that the client who owes a debt to the bank is no longer Max but the travel agency. The larger the bank, the greater the likelihood that the travel agency is also one of its clients.

If the 1 million euro is transferred to an account at another bank, Max's bank has to adjust its balance sheet. Of course not until the end of the day when numerous transfers between his bank and the other bank will have occurred. If nevertheless an imbalance remains, this is not really a problem. Max's bank will get a loan on the interbank market in the amount of the sum required. What makes this loan different from the money the bank holds in the checking accounts of their own clients is that it has to pay a small amount of interest.

Things will be more difficult for Max's bank if it has a bad reputation or if the entire banking system of a country has a bad reputation and his travel agency is located in another country. In that case it might not be possible to balance the amount through the interbank market, since foreign banks may not be willing to extend a loan to Max Lazybones' bank. But this would also not be a serious problem. In order to assist banks with such problems, the European Central Bank comes into play.

Since the financial crisis, the ECB has extended thousands of billions of euros in loans to European banks that were no longer able to get money on the interbank market or would have had to pay much higher interest rates. The ECB claims that all that money has not been created out of thin air, but extended to the banks only against collateral. In fact, banks have to provide bonds in order to receive ECB loans. But the standards for such bonds have been repeatedly lowered during the crisis. By now almost anything is accepted, from government bonds to packaged mortgages.

Without the support of the ECB, the banks in question would have lost their ability for the creation of unlimited amounts of money. They would have been able only to extend additional loans if someone had first deposited new money with them. The ECB provides such new money by accepting a whole range of financial products not only as collateral but also by directly buying them. If the seller is a bank, it is directly credited in its account with the Central Bank. If the seller is a capital fund or a firm, the bank will receive the money as a deposit in the fund's or firm's account. Currently 60 billion euros per month are made available to banks in this way.

Theoretically, all banks in Europe have sufficient opportunities to expand their loan business. It is indeed what they do, but they do not extend loans where it would make sense, i. e. in the real economy. Actors in the real economy, especially in crisis-ridden countries, continue to face great difficulties in receiving new loans or even just extending old ones. This fact is often greatly lamented, but the reasons are obvious. We have now reached a point where it is becoming clear why Max Lazybones would have probably never received a 1-million euro loan to go on vacation in the Maldives. In all likelihood the bank would not have trusted him ever to pay it back.

Bubble instead of small business loans

Of course this is not to say that small and mid-sized entrepreneurs in general cannot pay back their loans. But there is a significant risk that a business plan will fail when it comes to investments in innovative products and technologies. If, in addition firms don't have sufficient collateral, they are unlikely to get any money from their bank. True, a bank can create its own money, but if the loan goes sour it has to deduct the full amount from its own capital. If all of this happens in an environment of economic crisis of the kind that caused havoc in Portugal or Italy, not to mention Greece, the banker who may be hiding lots of bad loans in his balance sheet will be even more concerned that a small enterprise will sooner or later go under. As a result, the bankers prefer to keep their coffers closed.

An additional drawback for the banks is that mid-sized enterprises tend to ask for relatively small sums. A financial deal in the billions has a much more favourable cost-benefit ratio for banks. What is more, banks can rely on the fact that when the next crash happens, everyone will be affected. In that case either they will once again be saved by the state or it will all be over anyway. But as long as the music keeps playing, you have to dance, as the boss of the powerful U.S. bank Citigroup remarked in July 2007.

Thus there are reasons why the ability of today's banking system to generate money and credit in a virtually unlimited fashion is above all financing new and increasingly larger bubbles on financial markets rather than constructive investments. The European Central Bank's policy has been widely criticized in light of the real economy's continuing undersupply with credit. It is a fact that if, after the crash of 2008 and the collapse of the European interbank market, the ECB had not intervened with billions of euros, the current bubbles on almost all asset markets would not have emerged. However, this would have made things even worse in the real economies of Southern Europe. Instead of a credit squeeze, we might have experienced a complete collapse of the credit system, and thus even more bankruptcies and higher unemployment.

The suffering of the Cypriots

A bank collapse would have massively interrupted the flow of payments. Precisely because nowadays more than 80 percent of the money we use to pay for our daily purchases and our rent is electronic money, the smooth flow of transactions depends on the stability of the banks. The Cypriots are the only ones in Europe so far to have experienced what it actually means for our electronic money legally to be a loan to the bank. It means that if this money is gone, the bank will be bankrupt. In Cyprus, even healthy firms were unable to pay their employees since failing financial institutions froze their wage accounts. The fear of such an event occurring is itself enough to destabilize an entire economy.

And this is the source of the banks' outrageous power. We are permitting the same institutions entrusted with vital economic functions such as payment transactions and the provision of loans to firms to make their largest profits in wild orgies of financial speculation, and since for both the same resource, i.e. electronic money, is needed, this has made us subject to blackmail. We subsidize outlandish betting outfits since, as a sideline—with insufficient effort and without enthusiasm—they are responsible for financing business investments and allowing us to pay for our shopping. In the words of Martin Hellwig, quoted above: It is like paying the chemical industry for polluting our rivers and forests because they use the same poison to produce small amounts of a vital medication.

Of course we can continue doing this. Alternatively, we could think about restructuring the polluters of our environment in such a way that they manufacture a great deal more of the medication without having an opportunity to do their most profitable business by polluting our environment.

8.3 Money is a public good

The core task of banks is to provide purchasing power for innovative economic development that will enhance our prosperity in an environmentally sustainable way. Neither more nor less. What would such a banking system look like?

We have demonstrated that money is not scarce since it doesn't cost anything, even though everything can be bought with it. Whoever has a licence to create money has an immense privilege vis-à-vis all other economic actors. However, even if in principle there are no limits to increasing the money supply, it nevertheless ought to be kept scarce. If too much money is pumped into an economy, growth in demand will outstrip supply, and prices will increase. At the same time, if crucial investments cannot be financed because the emission of loans is blocked, this will also produce a crisis. What ultimately matters most is the question of who receives loans for what purpose. If the money flows into useful technologies and innovative products, it will create corresponding value. If it flows into expanding consumption, this may boost an economy in crisis, but there is the danger of inflation. If too much credit goes to a small number of financially strong borrowers, the result will be debt pyramids, as in the case of U.S. mortgage loans that at some point will collapse.

Why should the provision of a good with such characteristics be left in the hands of private profit-oriented businesses? There are no good reasons. This is why, in the nineteenth century, banks lost the right to print money. The argument supporting this move was that the creation of money was a public task—an argument also made at the time by economists of the liberal school, who generally did not have a favourable view of state intervention.

Banks as monetary intermediaries?

Many people therefore see the central goal of regulation as making banks into what most of us assume they are, i. e. mere middlemen who collect money from savers and pass it on to firms. Regulation should then deprive banks of the power to create credit from nothing. They would only be able to pass on what they have previously received from savers.

The question is, would that make sense? Credit is additional purchasing power introduced into an economy. Saving means that someone temporarily foregoes their purchasing power. Does this imply that in a stable monetary system the extension of credit comes after saving? Certainly not. If a loan finances an investment that makes economic sense, the equivalent value of the money will be generated by the additional production thus made possible. There is no reason why production should be preceded by saving. In economic terms, investment generates savings, since money spent on investment goods cannot be spent on consumption. To achieve this, no one has first to carry money to the bank.

Frequently, those who ultimately finance investments by forgoing consumption are not even consulted. Thus, in almost all capitalist countries, wage earners have financed industrialization through their involuntary sacrificing of consumption. Whether in England in the nineteenth century or in South Korea in the twentieth century, it was always the state that made sure wages stayed low—and it would usually not do so by democratic means. Large profits as well as additional purchasing power created by banks through loans made it possible to finance an enormous volume of investment.

The same dynamic of course also exists in the opposite direction. Low investment reduces incomes and ultimately has a negative effect on saving. Not taking into account foreign trade, at the end of a year savings and investments in an economy are always equal. What matters is the dynamic *during* the year, which determines whether they are equally high or equally low. And there are strong reasons why both investment performance and saving will be the higher the more purchasing power for sensible investments is available, regardless of whether anyone has first deposited money in their savings account.

Capital originates in work

From a different viewpoint, this demonstrates once more the absurdity of the thesis that capital income without work is somehow economically necessary to motivate people to save and reduce consumption, thus supplying the economy with sufficient capital. This thesis is obviously nonsense insofar as capital formation is due to profits driven up by involuntary reductions in consumption, i.e. by workers' low wages. However, even if capital originates in banks creating purchasing power from nothing, thus financing investment, it is difficult to see why, after loans have been paid back, there is a legitimate claim to income without work in the form of dividends and other payouts proportional to the newly created capital. The value corresponding to the purchasing power created by banks emerges from new production and thus from the labour of those who do the work—from the manager and engineer to the unskilled worker.

As we have concluded in the first part of the book, capital therefore is the result of work rather than individual frugality. For most firms, the precondition for the formation of additional capital that makes investment projects possible is the purchasing power created by banks. Nowadays, such purchasing power is available only to those who already possess capital, since banks require a high degree of security. This is what makes capital ownership in the present system exclusive. Those who already own capital receive more, and not because they lead a frugal life of hardship and unstinting work.

Sovereign-money theory

Let's return to the monetary order. Most of the purchases that used to be done in cash now use electronic money. There are even discussions about abolishing cash money altogether. If we want to have banks act as mere money brokers, we need to take away their power to create electronic money, just as in the past they lost the right to print money.

Technically that's not much of a problem. All of us, citizens and firms, would no longer have our checking accounts with private banks but directly with the central bank. As a result, the money in our checking accounts would no longer be a loan to a private bank. If a bank went bankrupt, this would affect only our savings, but not the money in our interest-free checking accounts. As savers we would become once again very attractive to the banks which, reduced to the role of brokers, would need our money to do business. It would be the end of the era of zero-interest savings accounts. There would have to be incentives for us to move secure money from our checking accounts to a less secure savings account with a private bank.

Bank loans would originate in savings only. The only institution with the right to create money from nothing would be the central bank. A group of economists who call themselves "sovereign-money theorists" advocate this model. Most of them propose that the central bank put additional money into circulation by providing it to the state to finance sensible projects. The license to print money always implies that someone will be able to make a profit without significant costs. That someone would no longer be the banks, but the state. This is the most attractive aspect of the proposal advanced by the sovereign-money school, and we will return to it later.

At first glance this concept seems to be convincing. The fact that everyone would have access to a secure account would be an improvement over the current situation. Upon further inspection, however, there are problems. There are reasons to assume that the credit supply of the real economy might suffer if banks were only allowed to issue savings-based loans. Profit-oriented banks at any rate would charge their lenders in addition to the higher interest rates the banks are paying to savers. The selection process would become even tougher. It is all too predictable that, compared to today, more investment projects would be rejected. Under these conditions, financing prospects for risky innovations would be even worse. The same applies to smaller firms, which always represent a greater risk to lenders than established corporations.

Bank runs and government guarantees

The argument that under such conditions private banks would collapse is unconvincing. A bank collapse would still affect the savings deposited in the bank. As soon as some event were to call a bank's stability into question—justified or not—people would start liquidating their savings and moving them to their checking accounts. In the system described above, this is all it would take to push a bank into insolvency. It means that simply shifting money from savings to checking accounts would have the same effect as did the bank run in Greece in June 2015, when everybody wanted cash. Under normal conditions—which did not obtain in Greece at the time—a central bank would just print more money in response to increasing demand for cash. In a sovereign money system, the central bank would be forced to compensate the bank in question for the withdrawal of savings. If the central bank fails to do that, the bank will collapse and savers will lose their money.

Why would anyone in such a system choose to hold their money in insecure savings accounts when they could safely keep it in an account with the central bank? Someone interested in investing 20,000 euros will, at a 3 percent interest rate, make 600 euros in the first year. A nice little sum, but hardly enough to risk savings intended for emergencies. Of course it is possible that interest rates may rise. But what does this entail for the credit supply of firms? And once the first bank has collapsed, with small investors losing their savings, millions of bank customers would liquidate their savings accounts at private banks. The only way to prevent such bank runs would be a public savings insurance of the kind that exists in Germany up to 100,000 euros. But a state guaranteeing by law the debts of private financial institutions has little to do with a market economy. Public savings insurance, however, we can safely assume, would constitute a significant incentive to keep completely insolvent banks alive through central bank loans.

Financial alchemists at work

Perhaps even more importantly, it should be remembered that until 1929, the cash monopoly of central banks did not prevent banks from financing an enormous stock market boom even though at the time there was no electronic money in today's sense. But the banks didn't need this. Even within the framework of a sovereign money system, it is possible for a bank to generate money from nothing if the recipient is credited the amount in a fixed-term deposit account rather than in a checking account. A certificate of these deposits could then be used for financial business.

It would be naive to assume that banks with access to a virtually infinite variety of derivatives would not find ways to create and bring into circulation credit money from nothing—above all for speculative purposes. Just as today's equity capital rules are circumvented through special derivatives, in a sovereign-money world hordes of financial alchemists would be devoted to the task of figuring out new derivative constructs in order to finance excessive financial deals under new conditions. And they would succeed.

While the ideas of the sovereign money theorists go in the right direction, they don't go far enough. It is not enough to scare the ghost into temporary hiding with holy water and spells. It has to be put back in the bottle. And the bottle has to be sealed permanently. In less metaphorical terms, an industry in which firms are not allowed to go bankrupt since that would have fatal consequences for the economy, while at the same time these firms can survive only with guaranteed state liability, should simply not be in private hands.

The market doesn't work for public goods

Money is a *public good*. Public goods are not suitable for the market. More specifically, there is no functioning market for them. A corporation manufacturing bad cars will sooner or later disappear from the market. A corporation producing bad financial products will become more and more powerful and eventually fill the post of U.S. Secretary of the Treasury. That's the difference. The money supply for the economy does not belong in the sphere of profit-oriented private enterprises, but in the hands of institutions oriented toward the public good, chartered by the government and subject to strict rules. It's basically the same as with water supply, hospitals, local transport, and many other public services. They can be privatized, but no one should be surprised if subsequently they no longer function properly.

The opposite of private providers is not simply government. There have been public banks with business models similar to those of private banks, as well as enterprises in other sectors that were state-owned but behaved like private profiteers. In Germany, there were *Landesbanken* (state banks located in the individual states of the Federal Republic), just like the *Deutsche Bahn* (German Rail) in rail transport, who eventually behaved in that way. However, this was not the case from the beginning. In its earlier life under the name of *Bundesbahn*, small towns still had their own railway connection, and its workers had no reason to strike. At the time when *Landesbanken* were simply clearinghouses for savings banks, with a responsibility for financing larger public and private investment projects, they made an important contribution to the economy. Eventually rules were relaxed in both sectors, and achieving the highest possible return became the supreme goal of these enterprises. It marked the end of their public mission and their commitment to the general good.

The 3-6-3 rule

The business model of savings banks and cooperative banks represents a model for the financial sector that makes sense. These banks finance the regional economy and offer secure investment opportunities for small savers. At one time their model was called the 3-6-3 model. In the morning they take in money at 3 percent, at midday they lend it at 6 percent, and since they have little other business, bank managers are on the golf course by 3. Basically this simple model describes how banks should function, though of course it doesn't have to be golf that's on the agenda in the afternoon.

Even savings banks and cooperative banks are not protected against the negative developments of the financial system as a whole. They too sold obscure financial products to their clients. They too provide poor loan opportunities for innovative young entrepreneurs. And they too don't pay their savers any interest on new deposits, whereas interest rates on loans for small businesses and overdrafts are significantly above 6 percent. These problems, however, can only be fixed with the help of a new framework and changed rules of the game for the entire financial industry.

Small is beautiful

The goal is thus a financial sector composed of small-sized units with a public mission which, while not profit-oriented, covers it own costs, providing the public good of *money* in such a way that the economy can develop in keeping with political priorities. The central actors of the financial order proposed here would be *common-good banks*. Common-good banks are primarily regional banks that conduct business only in a circumscribed territory, being familiar with the firms as well as local conditions. In addition, there should be a number of larger institutions that would function as clearinghouses, while also financing larger private or public investment projects. Their radius of action should not exceed the national scale.

Common-good banks are generally not permitted to do business with financial institutions that are not themselves common-good oriented. Finally, the common-good financial sector includes the central bank as the ultimate credit source for common-good banks, maintaining their liquidity and the cash supply. The central bank also acts as the government financier, with an eye not only to stable prices, but also a stable, innovative economy with a high level of investment and full employment.

The shrinking of banks and their business radius is of central importance. In order to avoid chain reactions, it is necessary to smash the chain. This is significantly more promising than trying to regulate and thus stabilize the banking industry across borders. History has demonstrated that the best way of ensuring that there will be no adequate regulation is to regulate only what different states can agree on. The smallest common denominator is always a weak one, as Hayek already pointed out. From the start, the EU financial market was a deregulation project in the interest of large banks. For the same reason, with respect to re-regulation in response to the most recent crisis, Europe has failed even more than the United States, which managed to impose at least some restrictions. If we want better rules, it is best to introduce them at the national level. If gradually other countries follow suit because it proves to be a better solution, an adequate financial architecture will eventually emerge in all of Europe. If we only regulate what EU members can agree on from the start, the goal will never be reached.

Capital controls are necessary

A monetary order for the common good can only be maintained if strict controls on capital transactions with other currencies exist. We have seen how the gold standard has restricted the scope for government policies, ultimately subordinating them to the interests of those who move the big money on an international scale. Even without the gold standard, free capital movement means that the value of a currency can be pushed up or down irrespective of real economic developments—depending on whether a country's policies are approved or disapproved by big money players. As Robert Stiglitz, winner of the Nobel Prize for Economics, has pointed out, the global freedom of capital basically does not generate any efficiencies. The only "benefit" is a significant weakening of the employees' position, since wage reductions, just like low capital taxes, can be extorted by threatening divestment.

There are many examples for this. French President Francois Mitterrand, who in the serious economic crisis of the early 1980s wanted to pursue Keynesian policies, and who with these instruments avoided the French economy's slide into negative growth rates, was ultimately defeated by speculation against the Franc. He either had to accept a radical devaluation and leave the European Currency System, or give up his Keynesian policies. Mitterrand opted for the latter.

On a global scale, massive capital movements have occurred for many years that are unrelated to the financing of world trade but instead result from interest rate differences, among other things. So-called carry trades exert pressure towards currency appreciation on currencies with higher interest rates, making exports from such countries more expensive and thus damaging their economies. Sudden policy reversals may result in extreme drops of the exchange rate, a credit squeeze, and bank collapse, thus causing even greater crises.

Gang of technocrats and euro dictatorship

Exchange rates should no longer be left to speculation, according to one of the objectives for the introduction of the euro. However, the idea of a common transnational currency has not lived up to expectations. A common-good oriented monetary order presupposes that there is a common political order with authority over its money and with the freedom to decide how to use it. In other words, a currency should be confined to a space that can be democratically controlled. The Eurozone cannot be democratically controlled, it does not even have democratic institutions. We have experienced how in a crisis euro countries with elected governments were disempowered by a technocratic gang composed of the EU Commission, European Central Bank, and IMF, and were forced to adopt policies that made the crisis worse and massively increased inequality. This gang was able to proceed much more ruthlessly than any elected government could have, since the population of the countries in question had no way of controlling or replacing them. Normally, we call such circumstances a dictatorship.

This applies not only to Greece. Spain, Portugal, and Ireland, and even Italy and France, have for some time not had any real freedom to choose their own policies. The events of the early summer 2015 could be repeated in any other euro country as soon as a government is elected that wants to set priorities deviating from neoliberal policies. The current plans for stabilizing the Eurozone will result in an even greater degree of de-democratization. In future, even in the absence of an acute crisis, Brussels technocrats may have the power to intervene in fiscal and tax policies, and even in the wage determination process, of individual euro countries.

"Restricting the room to act …"

This is precisely what the neoliberal fundamentalist Friedrich August von Hayek (1899–1992) had in mind—i. e. restricting democratic control over economic policy—as being the great advantage of a transnational currency. "With a common currency unit the room for action that central banks are given will be restricted at least as much as under a strict gold standard—perhaps even more … " he wrote in one of his essays in *Individualism and Economic Order*. In fact, in the nineteenth century, tariffs and other protectionist measures were available that are not possible within the EU. Having a currency without a state and at the same time free trade and free capital flows ultimately makes democracy impossible.

Some are calling for a democratization of the Eurozone. But that doesn't appear to be a promising project. All past attempts to establish supra-state institutions that would be democratically legitimated and workable have failed. The Brussels club of lobbyists is simply too removed and not transparent for Europe's citizens. People barely know the individuals in charge there and do not speak their language. A parliament elected by a mere 30 percent of its citizens will never become a democratic authority.

De-industrialization and a lost generation

It would therefore be a better idea to give democratic states their own currency back and introduce capital controls on currency exchange. This means that trade is financed but speculation is not. Under such conditions exchange rates would come under pressure in case of actual imbalances in the real economy. There would be an opportunity for adjustment by way of revaluation or devaluation. This would clearly be better than the straightjacket of the euro which does not permit use of this safety valve.

The alternative would be the continuation of the current situation. De-industrialization, mass unemployment, and extremely high youth unemployment at rates between 40 and 60 percent in practically Europe's entire South, including Italy, have brought declining wages, stagnating economic performance, growing poverty, and the emigration of the most qualified. Those who deprive national economies in the corset of a permanently overvalued currency of the opportunity to ever experience an economic recovery should not be surprised if, as in France, an increasingly strong far right will offer to solve the problem in its own nationalist way. This, however, would mean the end not only of the euro, but of Europe as a whole.

Keynes's Bancor Plan as a European currency system

As its point of departure, a functioning European currency system could use the Bancor Plan that Keynes developed as a draft for the Bretton Woods system. In such a system, the euro would be the anchor currency to which all other currencies would be pegged by fixed exchange rates which, however, could be changed if necessary. National central banks would guarantee exchange at these rates. Capital controls would pre-empt capital movements not based on real commercial transactions.

In such a system, long-term deficits and surpluses may occur if there are national divergences in productivity or wage trends—a probable development. European countries differ from each other not only in terms of culture and mentality, but also in terms of systems of trade union organization and other traditions of labour struggle. The period since the introduction of the euro has demonstrated that even under pressure of a common currency, these differences cannot be eliminated, which at any rate would not be beneficial.

A functioning European currency system with fixed exchange rates requires an institution that can finance deficits and surpluses in the short term and up to certain limits—the role the IMF was to play in Keynes's original plan. The ECB could take on this role today. If there are excessive or long-term deviations from balanced terms of trade, Keynes proposed that countries with surpluses and countries with deficits should both be penalized. These penalties would increase with the size of the imbalances. Penalties could be avoided if the country in question revalues or devalues its currency. Such a system would link democratic sovereignty over national money with a sufficient degree of exchange rate stability.

Those who believe that such a domestically oriented financial sector would threaten the future of a strong export economy such as Germany should revisit the post-war period. In order to finance exports, you don't need bank branches in Singapore, Panama, or Delaware. And since a country that is a strong exporter should in any event aim for equally large imports, there will be no need for extensive capital movements. A balanced trade account means just that, i. e. that exports and imports balance each other out. In contrast to most economists today, the head of the liberal Freiburg School, Walter Eucken, was aware that "[e]very export that does not make possible imports of at least the same value is harmful to the supply of goods."[90] It would thus be in the well-considered self-interest of surplus countries like Germany to increase their imports.

Financial check-up

All kinds of financial dealings and financial papers will have to pass a financial check-up. Only transactions that have a demonstrable use in the real economy will be licensed. Everything else will be prohibited. A non-profit institution should make the decisions. Its experts would receive a higher salary than top bankers and would therefore not be corruptible by the prospect of a lucrative banking job. This will not be excessively expensive since in common-good banks, no one will earn more than a director of a savings bank does today. A financial system that no longer makes outrageous profits will no longer be able to pay million-dollar salaries. This may sound antiquated and very boring, but it is exactly what we need: solid, steady banks rather than overexcited gambling casinos.

What matters is that society re-establishes its authority over the conditions of credit. It is the task of democracy to decide which sectors, technologies, and innovations should receive preferential financing. Those shocked by such a display of mistrust in "the market" should acquaint themselves with the history of countries like Japan, South Korea, or China. Successful economies have never left crucial decisions on credit to bankers but have established their own framework. When they stopped this practice, it was usually also the end of their period of success.

Successful credit allocation

Until the early 1980s Japan had a kind of planned economy in the form of the Ministry for International Trade and Industry (MITI), which issued quite specific instructions on priorities and product development. In addition, the central bank exercised credit control by directing individual banks on the extent of credit and the preferred industries to be financed. In this way, the country's export economy and semiconductor industry received preferential support. South Korea copied this model in the 1960s and 1970s, achieving a similar degree of success. In 1993, a World Bank study on the economic miracle in the Far East came to the conclusion "that state intervention for the purpose of credit allocation has played an essential role in attaining superior economic performance."[91] By that point in time, the Southeast Asian countries as well as Japan had largely abandoned this model. In China, on the other hand, state development banks continue to play a key role in the selection of prioritized technologies and economic sectors.

If, in the future, we want to have an economy based on green energy and integrated processes, we need to provide extensive earmarked funds for research into and the application of innovative technologies that can move us closer to this goal. And if we want a flexible, competitive economy, it is necessary to direct banks to provide a minimum level of loans to new entrepreneurs and set a target for loans to small and medium-size enterprises. That the market is incapable of doing this on its own has been sufficiently demonstrated. The final decision who will receive credit and who will not will lie with the bank, assuming this will once again be a genuine local bank with knowledge of the enterprises in its region—rather than leaving the decision up to some distant central office or an algorithm producing firm ratings based on untransparent standards.

If many young and innovative firms are financed, this means that the number of loan defaults will go up. The venture capital market in Silicon Valley assumes a failure rate of 90 percent for start-ups. Nine out of ten firms receiving financing are thus expected to fail. The problem with innovative projects is that no one can know ahead of time which will be the nine failures and which one the success. Investors calculate that a firm that does not go bankrupt within ten years will yield a twenty-fold return on the initial investment. This means that in spite of the failures, the investor will have doubled her risk capital.

On account of the peculiarities of digital business models, this calculation has frequently worked out. For other industries, however, it would be an absurd calculation, since a bank loan could not yield a twenty-fold return in ten years. On the other hand, an anticipated failure rate of 90 percent seems extremely high even for innovative projects. If we assume a failure rate of 50 percent, then a 10-year bond would break even at an interest rate of 7 percent.

More important, even if in the model proposed here the banks had to write off a larger number of investment loans than today, this would be more than offset by the absence of bad financial loans and other absurd financing schemes such as those leading to mortgage bubbles. Credit control would also be beneficial for the real estate market, since loans to the mortgage industry could be limited before the boom has even started. Similarly, it would be possible to intervene by giving preferential financing to single-family dwellings or rent-controlled units. Ultimately, banks that are satisfied with low profits could better deal with a larger number of bad loans. If the result is a more innovative and productive economy, this might be a price worth paying.

Innovation as risk

We should keep firmly in mind that money does not cost anything. Money is purchasing power, and ultimately society has the power to decide for what purposes it does and does not want to provide money. A loan gone bad means that additional purchasing power has gone into circulation without creating equivalent value. The investment has not increased society's prosperity. If this happens on a large scale, it can result in inflation. But banks always finance successful projects as well. So there is definitely room to take the risk of financing eventual failures since repayment of the loan plus interest removes more purchasing power than was initially created.

Such a model implies that banks may be involved in ventures in which making a loss is part of their calculation. It would be the task of management to keep losses of this kind limited. For a bank this entails that, when extending loans, it needs to select a wide range of projects, and on much broader scale than today. There can be no financial system in which every idea receives financing. However, we should create conditions in which a much larger number of innovative projects get a chance. In individual cases, a bank may still make a bad choice and get into trouble. If as a result it requires state aid in order to be stabilized, our taxes would at least be paying for the innovation power of our economy rather than the insatiable financial gambling of investment bankers. That would make a significant difference. In addition, any profits that common-good banks make will belong to the public.

Central banks as state financiers

As we have seen in previous sections, an economy's capacity for innovation depends not only on the financing of innovative young entrepreneurs, but also on publicly funded research and development activity. Many innovations that young entrepreneurs have launched on the market were first developed in public research institutions.

Yet successful public research requires that universities and research institutes don't degenerate into low-wage zones. Creativity is not enhanced by researchers having to worry about their contracts being extended every two years. The fundamental condition for an innovative economy therefore is a state that has stable financial resources at its disposal. While taxes should finance normal state expenditures from welfare to the state bureaucracy, economically relevant research and public investment could be financed by creating additional purchasing power.

In contrast to other banks, a central bank is not only able to extend loans. It can bring money into circulation without loans as well. Within reason and according to clear rules, the central bank should make use of this right by helping to finance the state. Basically the same applies here as it does for loans to the real economy. To the extent that the state uses central bank money to finance investments that will increase our prosperity, the money will create its own equivalent value, and there will be no threat of inflation. In contrast to loans, the central bank's direct creation of money does not create any debt and does not require interest payments. More money is simply put into circulation. This can also make sense in economic crises, since money that goes to the government—in contrast to the billions in loans extended by the European Central Bank today which only feed the banks—would contribute directly to the real economy in the form of additional demand.

Free lunch

At first glance, the idea that the state should receive money that no one pays for might appear a bit strange. There is no such thing as a free lunch, as economists like to remind us. Which means that in the economy, nothing is for free. This also applies to economic goods. But it does not apply to money. Since money does not cost anything, those providing it can demand goods without first receiving purchasing power from anyone. The kings and rulers of old gladly took advantage of this by putting into circulation coins with a material value significantly lower than their face value. Problems arose whenever the ruler used this privilege of coinage with excessive enthusiasm, thus creating a growing amount of coins in a stagnating economy. That's when coins were devalued, first in international exchange and subsequently in their domestic purchasing power. The creation of new money works only within narrow limits if the currency is to remain relatively stable.

Things would become dangerous if a central bank kept pumping the same amount of money into the economy regardless of whether there was an economic boom or crisis, or if the government used the money for expenditures that failed to generate any additional production or value, such as when political rulers line their own pockets or buy warships. But with proper regulation, such misuse could be monitored and prevented more easily than is possible today. True, central banks today are not permitted to give loans to the government, yet private banks do excellent business by creating money out of nothing, charging states hefty interest rates for lending them that money. As long as banks have faith in the solvency of a particular state, its corrupt political elites and warships will be generously financed. The market has never prevented this from happening.

Government bonds instead of money for gambling

In addition to new money from the central bank that should only be available in a limited fashion, it would certainly make sense to finance public investment by offering savers direct investment opportunities, e.g. in the form of government savings bonds. For citizens, these would be secure investments with moderate interest rates, and for democracy it would be a much better way of financing government deficits than current government securities. For simply placing the latter, investment banks make a profit, while in addition giving themselves the power to put pressure on governments of which they disapprove. Other than financial gamblers, no one needs public debt securities for use as play money on international financial markets. Like other securitizations, tradable government securities are completely superfluous. If a state is no longer able to go into debt abroad, this will reduce not only its dependency but also its opportunity to go into debt beyond what its economy can support. Both would represent progress.

The question remains how the transition from the current monetary order sketched here can be achieved. How do we get from today's casino and its betting outfits to a common-good oriented banking system?

This is actually much easier than it may initially appear. Every bank should be free to reorganize as a common good bank and to abide by the rules governing common-good oriented banks. Its legal form might be that of a common good corporation, as suggested in the next chapter. Under present conditions, institutions under public law and cooperative institutions would be compatible with this model, whereas joint-stock companies would not.

Rules for a market economy

All banks that want to remain private and continue to work for profit will be released onto the free market. This means that there will no longer be any state liability for their capital owners, and there will be no legally guaranteed deposit insurance for their investors. Private banks will no longer have access to loans from the central bank and will lose their right to create electronic money. In order to issue loans, they will need savings deposits for a minimum term, or they will have to issue and sell bonds. The assets of their owners will be held liable for their business activities. Anyone is free to deposit their money in these banks, and the banks can do with it what they wish within the law.

These rules are not particularly onerous, they are simply rules of the market economy. They would result in similar business conditions in the banking sector that apply to all enterprises in the regular economy. Some private banks will survive in this environment. In the United States and in the United Kingdom, investment banks used to exist that were set up as full-liability partnerships, operating on more modest scales, and specializing in certain types of financial transactions such as the emission of shares and bonds. The state should leave banks alone that are able to survive in this way.

The Icelandic model

All banks not able to survive under such conditions—which will probably include most large banks like Deutsche Bank—will need post-bankruptcy restructuring, decontamination, and downsizing. The small state of Iceland offers a model which, in contrast to all other European countries, was adopted after the start of the financial crisis, allowing it to keep public debt within strict limits. Following this model would mean breaking up each bank into a "good bank" for all checking accounts, savings, and other deposits, as well as all recoverable loans and accounts, and a "bad bank" for bad loans and questionable financial instruments.

In order to write off bad loans, the shareholders of the old bank will carry primary liability, next come the owners of equity-type instruments, and finally the holders of bank bonds. In this way, losses can be liquidated. By including bank bonds and other financial instruments, offshore assets will be drawn into the liability pool, since such instruments tend to be held by international financial institutions and funds. They are also the front for the global financial elite's money stashed away in the world's tax havens.

Basically, this model means securing the assets of the middle class, while the assets of the upper class will pay for the dysfunctional developments of the past decades in the financial sector. This is only fair, since the upper class exclusively benefited form these developments. We can assume that the assets of the wealthiest will be more than enough to cover liability. Fifty percent of all financial assets, or 80 percent if offshore assets are included, today belong to the richest 1 percent.[92] In order to secure the financial assets of 99 percent of the population, including life insurance and pension savings, only 20 percent of loans, papers, and other claims in today's financial system would have to be recoverable. Notwithstanding the shady business practices in the industry over past decades, the share of financial junk will certainly lie significantly below 80 percent.

The good bank would be transformed into a common good bank. This transition would be largely without cost for the public sector. The more countries decided in favour of a common-good oriented banking sector, the better. Theoretically, the model proposed here could be introduced in Germany only or in a small number of European countries. For all countries embarking on this route, this would mean not only a significant gain in innovation capacity and efficiency but also in democracy. A sovereign monetary order is the precondition for state sovereignty. And only a sovereign state can be run democratically.

9. RETHINKING PROPERTY

9.1 Property theories since Aristotle

The first man, who, after enclosing a piece of ground, took it into his head to say, "This is mine," and found people simple enough to believe him, was the true founder of civil society. How many crimes, how many wars, how many murders, how many misfortunes and horrors, would that man have saved the human species, who pulling up the stakes or filling up the ditches should have cried to his fellows: Be sure not to listen to this imposter; you are lost, if you forget that the fruits of the earth belong equally to us all, and the earth itself to nobody![93]

Jean-Jacques Rousseau, author of this impassioned plea that can be found in his *A Discourse Upon The Origin And The Foundation Of The Inequality Among Mankind*, was no opponent of private property. He knew that life was better in a society in which not just anyone can harvest your carefully tended strawberry field, ride your horse, or take your grandmother's family jewels. But he also knew the difference between owning objects of daily use and owning land. In Rousseau's times, farmland was the most important resource of a national economy. Those who owned a lot of land could command the work of others since they were dependent on this resource. Landowners were thus able to make large profits without working themselves. Rousseau disapproved of this kind of property that made it possible to profit at the expense of others.

Finding the right measure

Rousseau's view is part of a long tradition in Western thought. Aristotle defended the legitimacy of private property in principle, but only to the extent that it served security and personal development. In this sense, there was a limit to how much property one should own, above which it ceases to be a *good*. The true task of the economic arts was finding the proper measure and right kind of property. Those, on the other hand, who valued goods solely in terms of their monetary value and who pursued the goal of a potentially unlimited increase in wealth, the Greek philosopher—much like the French enlightenment philosopher Rousseau—considered to be rather pathetic creatures.

Rousseau did not live to experience the French Revolution, but he could have felt vindicated. Questions of land ownership, the rights of owners, and the legitimacy or illegitimacy of government intervention in free property ownership were at the centre of political conflicts after the storming of the Bastille. In August 1789, the French National Constituent Assembly proclaimed its *Declaration of the Rights of Man and of the Citizen*. The Declaration defined as "natural and inalienable human rights" "the right to liberty, the right to property, the right to security, and the right to resistance against oppression". A special article, Article 17, is dedicated to property as an "inviolable and sacred right", that no one can be deprived of private usage "unless under the condition of a just and prior indemnity."

The liberation of landed property from feudal fetters was one of the first acts of the French Revolution. Liberation of landed property meant that henceforth everybody was free to buy, sell, or mortgage land. Feudal authority and other feudal obligations were abolished, and lords had no more responsibility for dependants who were now free peasants. The old feudal taxes did not disappear but for the most part were transformed into land rents. Only church property and the property of emigrant nobility were confiscated by the state, subsequently to be sold to the highest bidders.

Right of use and misuse

The laws of the French National Assembly made possible owner-ship of land, in the sense of the concept of property later defined by Article 544 of the Napoleonic Code: as the right to use a thing without any restrictions and to dispose of it. This expressly included the right to misuse one's property, to use it for usury, the formation of monopolies, and speculation, and even the right to destroy it.

Private property as such had existed for a long time. Even in the darkest middle ages, anyone could buy a chicken or an axe, which would thus become their property and could not simply be taken away by others. If the peasant wanted to slaughter the chicken or toss the axe in the lake, he was free to do so. Different rules applied only to the crucial productive resource of the time, which was land.

Historically, the Romans were the first to consider land as something that could be freely bought and sold just like other mobile objects or slaves. They already defined property as a bundle of rights, the most important of which consisted in owners being able to use things in any way they desired and to exclude others from having any influence over them. An owner may use his property, sell, mortgage and bequeath it. No one has the right to interfere, not even the state. Like some American neocons today, the Romans original-ly considered imposing taxes as an inadmissible encroachment of property rights. In many respects, today's civil law goes back to the old Roman law. Interestingly, the Romans used the same word for property as for rule: *dominium,* derived from *dominus,* master. An owner was thus a master.

New Masters

As masters—this is precisely how the landowners in post-revolu-tionary France acted after they were freed from all former ties and obligations. In stark contrast to the hopes of peasants, property rights resulted above all in massive concentration of land ownership. True, French peasants now had the right to take over the land previously held by feudal lords and transform it into their own property. However, they had to pay a transfer fee of twenty times the amount they used to pay in annual taxes. For most of the peasants, the right to ownership therefore existed on paper only, since they had no opportunity to raise the money that would have turned them into landowners.

In 1792 and 1793, large producers and wholesalers were hoarding food in order to push up prices, thus causing famines and riots in the cities. In the National Assembly, a controversy started over what should be accorded higher value—the right to life or the inviolability of property. The Girondists defended the latter, while the Jacobins demanded government-imposed upper limits on food prices, an obligation to sell food, and laws protecting society from misuse of private property. Others went even further, claiming equality of ownership, redistribution of land, and a general law against owning more than was necessary for the satisfaction of one's own needs.

The questions that occupied French politicians at that time are relevant to this day. Is property an inviolable human right that primarily needs protection from state interference? Or, on the contrary, is a free state obligated to defend the liberty of citizens against the arbitrary power of large landowners? When is property an indispensable tool for self-development and when does it mean "the power to produce without work"[94], as the French social theorist Pierre-Joseph Proudhon argued in his book *What is Property?* What property is legitimate, and what property is not? And why is it that some have so much more of it than others?

Property as a natural right

The English philosopher John Locke was among the first to come up with the idea of defining the right to property as a universal natural right, independent of any state laws. Locke lived in the seventeenth century and is considered one of the fathers of political liberalism. His starting point was the thesis that every human was the natural owner of his or her body, and thus of her abilities and physical efforts. Owning the product of one's labour was a *natural* consequence of this right. That is, those who turn an uncultivated piece of land not owned by anyone else into a field, applying industry and hard work, have the right to call this field their property and to enjoy its fruits.

Thus legitimate property is the result of work. That sounds attractive and revolutionary, particularly coming from a liberal. During Locke's lifetime in Europe, most people toiled on fields they did not own and the fruits of which they were not able to enjoy, just as today a majority work in companies they don't own and the profits of which flow to others. It was also evident in Locke's time that large holdings such as the nobility's huge feudal estates never came into existence as the result of their owners or even their ancestors ever having taken ownership of no-man's land through individual labour. Was Locke's theory demanding the expropriation of the nobility and the handing over of the land to the peasants?

Why don't you just leave

It did not. Locke instead produced a particularly cunning legitimation of the property status quo of his time. His labour theory of property applies only to the *state of nature*. With the introduction of money, we leave the state of nature. With the help of money anyone can acquire more property than they themselves can work, since this property can be increased by using paid labour. The more property one owns, the more people can be employed and the faster this property increases.

According to Locke, this property is nevertheless legitimate, since anyone who does not approve of the existing order and the large inequality that goes with it is free to emigrate to areas of the world where unowned land is still to be had, which through one's own labour can be turned into individual property. Thus no one has to toil on other people's land. Those who still do, do so voluntarily, thus accepting the existing order. So much for the argument of Locke, who believed he had thus solved a problem that had defeated social contract theorists such as Hugo Grotius: contracts are binding only for those who have consented to them. In order to legitimate the property system, it was therefore necessary to show that the underlying contract concerning *owning* and *not owning* had been entered into voluntarily by all, including those who were left with the worst outcomes.

Such supposedly unowned land existed primarily in North America, where the land taken from the indigenous population was distributed to the settlers. That property arose from one's own work was a personal experience for many. However, there was another reason why Locke's theory enjoyed such popularity on the North American continent. It provided a welcome justification for the forced displacement of aboriginal people. If property comes into existence only by someone cultivating a field, the North American Indians—like the aboriginal people of other continents—did not have any property. No sacred human right was therefore violated when they were deprived of the land on which they had lived and which had sustained them.

The disappearing commons

By the early nineteenth century, all the land in the United States had been appropriated by someone—the same was true for the rest of the world. This in fact undermined Locke's legitimation of the property status quo and its great inequality. There was no longer any place to emigrate for landless peasants or workers without capital as an alternative to selling their labour for meager wages.

Strictly speaking, the implication of Locke's theory under such conditions was that only property based on one's own labour could claim legitimacy by natural law. This would be in keeping with the original justification of human rights, the purpose of which was to protect the sphere of personal life from state interference and arbitrary authority rather than to protect social power. In reality, the theory of property as a human right preceding any public power and legislation was used as a mechanism to protect and defend precisely the property that could not be traced back to the individual work of its owner.

Property rights versus democracy

Starting in the nineteenth century, the hands of parliaments were tied and democratic decisions were overturned with reference to the inviolability of property and freedom of contract. In spectacular decisions, the U.S. Supreme Court time and again annulled State and Federal law which the judges considered to be in violation of the rights and liberties of economic property holders.

In this way, the Supreme Court declared as unconstitutional legislation against a monopoly of slaughterhouses, which was driving up meat prices, or the attempts of several states to restrict the ruthless exploitation of the railway monopoly and regulate railway prices. A Federal law designed to prohibit companies from discriminating against workers who were union members was rejected. The judges argued that this constituted an inadmissible interference in freedom of contract. A regulation restricting the daily working time of bakers to a maximum of ten hours as well as a minimum wage law for women were rejected for the same reason.

Personal property and economic property

Not until the twentieth century did the concept of economic property change, and along with it the way the law was applied. The old inviolability clause was replaced by the formula of a *property guarantee* and the principle of *social obligation*. "Property entails obligation, its use should also serve the public interest", according to the Basic Law, Germany's post-World War II constitution.

In a decision from 1979, Germany's Federal Constitutional Court explicitly recognized varying degrees of protection for private property, depending on whether property for personal use or extensive economic property is concerned. In a judgment on the question of co-determination (worker participation in decision-making) in enterprises, the judges explain: "In so far as the function of property is an element in securing an individual's personal freedom, it enjoys particularly broad protection... Conversely, the authority of legislation with respect to determining the substance and limits of protection varies in proportion to the social relationship and social function of a piece of property."

There is thus a distinction between *personal property* and its protection as an individual right and *property in social contexts*, which affects the rights of a large number of people. Property should be tied to obligations, but it can also destroy rights. According to the German Basic Law, this is where the state is called upon to intervene.

Protected power

In recent history, however, the state has frequently done the opposite. Jurisdiction as well has strongly supported the rights of the economically powerful. Over the past two decades, the European Court of Justice has suspended social legislation of individual member states in a large number of cases with reference to property rights and other economic rights. In Germany as well, the freedom of economic property owners is receiving preferential treatment.

When, in 2009, the economics minister Rainer Brüderle tried to start a debate on a law on decartelization in order to counteract massive processes of economic concentration, legal experts were quick to produce a report that simply declared such a law unconstitutional. State measures curtailing the entrepreneurial decisionmaking powers of shareholders, according to this legal opinion, represented undue interference in property rights.[95] The right to amass economic power as a constitutionally guaranteed fundamental right? The fathers of the Basic Law and the economists of the ordoliberal school must be turning in their graves. The project of decartelization at any rate was quickly filed.

Legitimate profit expectations?

Recent discussions about the protection of property are mostly about the protection of the power of corporations from employees or democracy. For example, in the fall of 2015, a strike by Lufthansa pilots was outlawed with the argument that it was not about wage rates but was directed against corporate strategy. Employees obviously should not involve themselves in a company's strategy, even if, as in the case of Lufthansa, this strategy was the setting up of a subsidiary designed to lower wage costs.

With the free trade agreements CETA and TTIP, the economic rights of owners are to be assigned an even higher priority over government legislation. In these treaties the duty to protect property is extended to include the owners' "legitimate profit expectations". Any law that reduces profit expectations in this way becomes a case of "nationalization" and is as such inadmissible. This would undermine the strengthening of regulations for environmental or consumer protection, protection against wrongful dismissal, or a significant increase in the minimum wage. The government is not necessarily forced to cancel the law in question, but instead has to pay corporations full compensation. The predictable result will be— indeed, is supposed to be—that no state, regardless what government is in power at the time, will be able to afford adoption of such expensive legislation.

Wage-dumping as a human right?

When a court can repeal laws with reference to individual rights, it presupposes that these are universal rights existing independent of any particular legal framework. Of course such rights do exist—the right to life, liberty, physical integrity, and security. But is it really a universal human right to be allowed to shut down a profitable enterprise in city X in order to resume production in city Y with cheaper workers? Or to saddle a corporation with constantly growing debt in order to increase the payout for shareholders? Or even to be shielded from a state seeking to strengthen employee protection or environmental laws?

As a matter of fact, property rights cannot be a right predating a state, since our very concept of property is defined by our laws. The object worthy of protection is something the lawmaker creates, which is why it has been constantly redefined. Today there are legally protected forms of "intellectual property" that our ancestors would have considered utterly absurd. While in the nineteenth century there were debates about whether or not it makes sense to have patents for technological inventions (German Chambers of Commerce at the time were opposed), today you can have microorganisms or gene sequences patented. Such property rights come into being as a result of legislation and legal practice, and it would of course be equally conceivable to have laws against making living nature the commercial property of particular corporations.

The same is true for the financial industry. In the United States, for a long time banks' over-the-counter trade in derivatives was not legally protected. Today it is, which is why we are now dealing with property rights. If those business transactions were considered superfluous, we could simply withdraw their legal protection again. What property is and what is a proper object of property rights is therefore highly controversial, with corresponding laws repeatedly subject to change.

Property as a convention

There were sound reasons why in the European Convention for the Protection of Human Rights and Fundamental Freedoms of 1950, property rights were relegated to a mere supplementary article.

In the UN Human Rights Convention of 1966, they are completely absent. In the eighteenth century, David Hume, philosopher and friend of Adam Smith, advocated a conception of property rights opposed to Locke's *natural rights*-based justification. For Hume property rights are simply the result of social conventions that emerged in the context of historical struggles and can be changed at any time. Thus for Hume there is no natural right, but rather a challenge for society to design property rights.

The Scottish philosopher argued in favour of designing a property order that advances the common good. Hume was not a particularly rebellious thinker, which is why in his view historically evolved property regimes should be respected as far as possible. His basic approach, however, is correct. What someone may call their property and how it can be increased is determined by laws. This includes tax laws. In a country with a high property tax, an owner is likely to have less money after ten years than in a country without property tax. For this reason tax laws cannot collide with property rights—they are part of them.

Property as performance motivation

The decisive question therefore is: Which property order will increase our prosperity and which property rights will damage it? There are good reasons to guarantee and protect, as a fundamental right, property that results from one's own work and constitutes an individual's personal sphere of life. This applies also to the free and arbitrary disposal of this property, assuming that third parties will not be harmed.

On the one hand, we are dealing with the private sphere of every individual in which the state is not allowed to interfere. On the other hand, there is a large number of examples for the fact that people who cannot be sure that the fruits of their labour will be protected against arbitrary seizure quickly lose the motivation to work. Adam Smith formulated this in drastic but correct terms: "A person who can acquire no property can have no other interest but to eat as much and to labour as little as possible."[96]

Property rights should protect one's private sphere rather than society's power structure. They should motivate effort, creativity, and performance rather than be an instrument for enrichment at the expense of others. Let's see to what extent the current property rights order is compatible with this principle.

9.2 Ownership without liability: the genius of capitalism

One of the most widely used justifications for the dynamism and irreplacability of capitalism rests on the argument that people are most committed when caring for their personal property. What belongs to them without anyone else having a say, what they may grow for their personal benefit, load up with debt at their own risk, and finally pass on to their children—this will be the object of their greatest determination, care, and commitment. It follows that if we want well-managed, successful enterprises, we must not under any circumstances call into question private economic ownership. Until 1989 in Eastern Europe and the Soviet Union, the argument continues, we saw what happened when the state or other forms of collective ownership take the place of personally responsible and liable owners—slovenliness, lack of economic discipline, and technological stagnation. And who would want to return to those conditions?

True, we don't want to go back in time. But this doesn't change the fact that the argument in defense of capitalism according to which the solely responsible owner-operator guarantees successful management and economic dynamism is mistaken. For if that were true, capitalism would have been a huge economic failure. It is true that the age of capitalism was preceded by the liberation of property from old feudal restrictions and dependencies as well as the legal guarantee of free enterprise. But the original contribution of capitalism was not that of free, fully accountable property, which already existed under Roman law. Capitalism's original contribution to property rights was limited liability ownership, such as incorporated companies and public limited companies enjoy—a somewhat peculiar property rights construction which guarantees owners full access to all profits made by the company while holding them liable for the risks they take only up to their initially invested capital.

Personal liability

The legal model operating under the heading of joint stock company is, on further inspection, a rather peculiar thing. Actors in a market economy are usually liable with all of their assets for any contractual obligations they enter into. Thus if I have incurred debt and can no longer make my payments, at some point the bailiff will show up at my door to check if I own any valuables that could be sold for the benefit of the creditor. Even if it is an heirloom with a high personal value for me, it will not make any difference.

If I act as an individual entrepreneur or set up a business partnership with others, the same rules apply. Let's assume that a young man full of ideas wants to open up a restaurant. He will rent the premises, buy the furniture, and hire a cook and three waiters. For this he'll use all his savings accumulated over several years, as well as a bank loan for his additional expenses—a loan for which he qualifies because he has just inherited a house from his uncle. If the venture fails, this will have serious consequences for the young man. Not only does he stand to lose the savings he invested, but he will be liable for the loan with all his assets, from his own car to the house he inherited. If that is not enough, he may have to work for years to pay back the bank, or until personal bankruptcy will finally allow him to make a new start.

The risk he is taking is therefore very high. On the other hand, if the young entrepreneur has made a lucky choice with his cook and the restaurant has been a success, all the profits will belong to him. The cook and the waiters receive a wage, but as the owner he may become quite wealthy. He can use the profits and an additional bank loan to open up more restaurants. He will be the owner and recipient of all the returns they generate. This is the case even though their success depends at least as much on his staff's performance as on his management skills. What would a restaurant be without skilled cooks and friendly waiters? Our young entrepreneur of course had the original idea, found a market niche, and chose the staff. He is responsible for keeping the place going, and he is liable for all its debts. If his successful run comes to an end, he may very quickly lose everything—not only his restaurants, but all of his assets. Unless our young entrepreneur is a gambler, he will be careful not to take on excessive debt.

Limited risk, unlimited profit

Things would be different if our young entrepreneur were really smart and set up a joint-stock company or corporation. He would have the same advantages. Strictly speaking, he would no longer be the owner of the restaurant—it is now owned by the corporation. But as its only shareholder, he controls everything that his cooks and waiters generate, minus the costs, and the same would be true for any additional restaurants. Thus he can increase his personal assets by releasing profits to himself, replacing his modest house with a villa on the lake and a yacht, and living a life of luxury. And if at some point his restaurant chain goes under, he will lose—nothing! Merely the relatively small amount he initially invested in the corporation in order to open the first restaurant is lost. In the meantime, of course, he has made that investment many times over. A pretty good setup.

Corporations—which includes joint-stock companies and limited liability companies—have, on the one hand, unlimited control of the profits generated by the business, while on the other, they carry the limited risk of losing the initial investment in case of bankruptcy. Once the capital contributors have recovered their initial investment, there is basically no further risk for them. In the worst case, they may lose the goose that lays the golden eggs, i. e. that is generating fresh profits all the time. Once shareholders or partners have the profits in their private accounts, they cannot be held liable in the case of future losses. Suppliers, creditors, and possibly society as a whole, will get the short end of the stick. Imagine if during the most recent financial crisis, the global financial elite had been held liable with their private assets! That would have reduced the wealth of the top 1 percent much more significantly than any property tax, and states would not have incurred billions in debt.

We are so used to limited liability for economic property that the question never arises, let alone do we call the principle into question. But on closer inspection limited liability is a contradiction in terms. That's why this legal institution was always rejected by consistent defenders of the market economy, from Adam Smith to Walter Eucken.

Parliamentary right of reservation concerning corporations

It did take quite some time for the corporation to become a generally available legal form of enterprise. The first share company in the world was the Dutch East India Company (VOC) established in 1602. This was by no means a normal commercial enterprise but rather a semi-state entity with a publicly guaranteed trade monopoly and quasi-state powers in the colonies. Following the model of the VOC, additional share companies were set up for the purpose of colonial trade in the sixteenth and seventeenth centuries. They had a special status and therefore also a unique legal form.

In general, until the nineteenth century share companies were permitted only for actual or presumed "public purposes". In addition to long-distance trade with the colonies, these included the construction of transport routes such as canals and railway lines. In England until 1844, parliament had to vote on the licensing of every share company. In the United States as well, the legislature reserved the right of control. It authorized concessions for particular commercial projects, such as the construction of a canal. The company was not permitted to be active in any other area, and the concession expired after a certain number of years.

Sold off by the owners

General permission to establish share companies had to wait until the nineteenth century. In the United States, the corresponding laws were adopted in 1811, in England in 1844. In Germany too, the law for share companies was liberalized in the nineteenth century, with the creation of an additional legal form, the limited liability company (GmbH), in 1892. There was a need for limited liability ownership because, contrary to a widely held myth, the owner-entrepreneur was in fact not the typical representative of capitalism.

As we saw in the chapter on "robber barons", industrialization quickly drove up the minimum of capital an enterprise needed in order to operate efficiently. This rapidly rising need for capital could only be provided by external financiers. To attract investment capital from third parties carrying full liability is difficult, since the risk for capital providers under these conditions is very high. In addition, there was a growing appetite for credit among rapidly expanding enterprises, which in case of bankruptcy threatened the owner with complete and life-long ruin.

Ernst Abbe, founder and head of the Carl Zeiss Foundation, which will be further discussed in the following section, noted the reaction to these challenges in the second half of the nineteenth century. "It has become an almost regular phenomenon in recent economic development that industrial enterprises, once they have passed a certain size, are sold off by their personal owners and ... usually transformed into share companies or other similar forms."[97]

Separating investor and entrepreneur

In the United States today, corporations have revenues five times those achieved by companies with full owner liability. In Germany as well, value creation in corporations exceeds value creation in personal liability companies many times over. The corporation is the typical ownership form of capitalism, since the separation of investor and entrepreneur is the typical form of doing business in this economic order.

Of course, not every corporation is managed by a non-owner. Among small and medium-sized enterprises, there are many owner-managed companies that take advantage of the benefits of this legal form, for instance in the area of taxation. For most small enterprises, however, limited liability is not helpful since banks will usually demand personal property as security. Only once the enterprise has grown and initial loans are paid off will the owner benefit from this peculiar legal construct that offers unlimited prospects for profit with limited risks of loss.

Leave the work to others

Globally, large enterprises almost exclusively take the legal form of corporation. In most of them, the large shareholders limit themselves to a controlling function. They are present at annual shareholder meetings or dominate the board of directors. This is where they decide on corporate strategy, instruct management, and exchange top personnel. The actual work of operational management is left to others.

The popular phrase "family business" may suggest intimacy and patriarchal obligations. But many enterprises that go by that name have little to do with actual family-managed firms. Family businesses exist in the artisanal sector, the restaurant sector, or in micro firms. With three exceptions, on the other hand, the CEOs of the 80 largest German companies that have majority family ownership are not drawn from the owner family. In large family-owned corporations, the owners tend not to get involved directly in management. Only among lower-ranked companies are CEOs or top management made up of members of the owner family. But even in that group it is not the rule. Even among the so-called "hidden champions" of the German economy, i. e. mid-sized companies that are market leaders in global niche markets, less than half are managed by their owners.

Family feuds as a business risk

Heirs limiting themselves to a controlling function, leaving operative management to professionals, help to facilitate the continued existence of the company. It would make little sense for highly gifted mathematicians to bequeath their university positions to their children. Similarly, it is unlikely that a company founder will raise children with the same exceptional abilities he possesses. True, it may happen in some cases, but the alternative of the firm declining will occur more frequently. And the larger the enterprise, the more demanding its management. It is a talent you have or you don't—it can't be learned.

It is therefore problematic if a company is passed on to heirs who are unwilling to accept this limitation, or warring heirs who all think they are destined to be the CEO. Incapable heirs or family feuds may destroy hundreds or even thousands of jobs. Tom A. Rüsen from the Witten Institute for Family Enterprises maintains that "about 90 percent of crises in family firms originate in family conflicts rather than in market conditions."[98] Roughly 80 percent of those are succession conflicts.

Control for personal benefit

Such conflicts of course may also occur in shareholders meetings or on the board of directors, with potentially equally damaging results. Giving up management does not mean that the owners lose their influence on the company. On the contrary, thanks to the legal form of corporation, they are able to exercise influence over much larger companies than their billion-dollar assets would otherwise allow them to do.

Under the headline of "New Germany Inc.", the business daily *Handelsblatt* recently discussed the fact that large shareholders from family dynasties continue to control many German corporations. The authors point out that "in almost half of the 30 blue chip corporations listed on the German Stock Market Index (DAX), there are anchor shareholders that practically single-handedly determine the fate of the corporation." *Handelsblatt* also noted the downsides of this feudal capitalism. Whether the model had positive or negative effects on the company depended on whether the interests of the firm and those of the family did or did not coincide. If they have the same interests, it'll work. "If large shareholders act completely in their self-interest, it's a curse."[99] Well, much the same was true for the old feudal lords.

In other EU countries as well, families control major parts of the industrial sector. The Wallenberg family, for example, controls one in three of Sweden's largest corporations, and in total about 40 percent of market capitalization of Swedish industrial enterprises. The family exercises this control exclusively through Investor AB, a corporation of which it owns half. The corporation as a legal form not only has the benefit of limited liability for the owners but, based on complex legal constructs, also provides the opportunity to directly dominate far more sectors of the economy than its own capital would allow them to do.

Owner Aladdin

Many companies today are owned by corporations, anonymous shareholders, or private equity firms. We've become used to the fact that not only individuals and families, but also hedge funds and other financial investors may be the owners of companies, trading them, buying and selling them as they see fit, or breaking them up and cannibalizing them. This is only possible thanks to the corporation as a legal form and should therefore not simply be taken for granted.

No more than 15 percent of shares listed on the DAX today are held by private individuals, while 70 percent belong to so-called institutional investors. They may be a front for family dynasties or just profit-obsessed financial vehicles from anywhere in the world. One large investor with shares in almost every DAX-listed company is the U.S. asset manager BlackRock, which has 6,000 high-capacity computers and a data analysis system by the name of Aladdin in charge of its portfolio decision-making.

This is what the responsible owners in today's capitalism look like—the kind that in the interest of innovation and successful management we supposedly couldn't do without. Already in the early 1940s, Schumpeter criticized that, with the advent of the corporation, "the traditional role of the owner and with it its specific ownership interest had vanished."[100] We should therefore stop rationalizing capitalism with the erroneous argument about the irreplaceability of the owner-entrepreneur who in large parts of the economy was phased out long ago.

Increasing concentration of economic power

The legal construct of the corporation is also responsible for the growing concentration of economic power, since it makes it possible to set up and oversee a large number of firms from a central locus of control. Without this effect, economic units today would be much smaller and competition between them more intense. It is admittedly true that industrial production as well as the delivery of many services have to occur on a large scale. However, the reach of today's global corporate giants significantly exceeds what is necessary to achieve economies of scale. The legal form of the corporation facilitates economic concentration simply by making possible the exchange of shares between companies. A personal liability company, on the other hand, would find it difficult to raise the capital needed to buy up a company with billions in revenue.

The corporate model also makes tax evasion and money-laundering easy, since it permits concealing ownership structures and setting up faceless foundations, investment firms, or offshore companies. To this day, the establishment of a European company register even just listing who are the economic actors legally in charge has failed—among other reasons because the German government blocked it. Obviously this is a way of obscuring and anonymizing economic power, which is very much in the interest of manufacturing, finance, and service industry oligarchs.

But is all of this desirable? Are ownership conditions of this kind in fact the precondition for a dynamic, innovative economy that increases prosperity for all—or do they not themselves constitute a major barrier? What would alternative arrangements look like? We will address these questions in the final section.

Companies owned by foundations

A foundation has a charter and manages an asset for a particular purpose. However, a foundation does not have owners. Companies that are completely in the hands of a foundation are thus companies without external owners. Someone of course oversees such companies, charting their strategy and hiring management. Frequently these are the heirs of the former owners who live on the money transferred to them by the foundation. In such cases, the foundation model simply reinforces the old feudal conditions and income flows. In some cases, however, things are different, as will be further explained below. The important point is: foundations demonstrate that control—in a positive sense and a negative sense—can also be exercised without ownership.

Many large multi-billion dollar corporations in Germany are nowadays in the hands of foundations. The Alfred Krupp von Bohlen und Halbach Foundation, which owns 25 percent of Thyssen-Krupp Inc. and has been in existence for half a century, or the Robert Bosch Foundation, which holds 92 percent of the shares of the Bosch Corporation. Also well known are the Bertelsmann Foundation as major shareholders of the Bertelsmann corporation and the Else Kröner-Fresenius Foundation, which owns almost one-third of shares of the medical technology and hospital corporation Fresenius.

But there are lesser known foundations owned by large companies with multi-billion dollar revenues. The Zeppelin Foundation, for instance, is a major shareholder of Germany's third-largest auto parts manufacturer, ZF, and the Mahle Foundation is owned by the Mahle Inc., one of the world's twenty largest corporations in the auto industry supply business. Then there is the Carl Zeiss Foundation, established in 1889 to administer the precision optics manufacturer of that name in Jena, the Montan Foundation Saar which controls the steel industry of the Saarland, the Diehl Foundation which among others owns a large arms manufacturer, the Körber Foundation which runs an international technology corporation, and many others. In the retail industry as well, the foundation model is flourishing. Aldi Süd and Aldi Nord, as well as the discount retailer Lidl and the drugstore chain dm, are today owned by foundations.

Personal benefit instead of collective benefit

Some of these foundations carry the label "charitable", and a small number of their founders were in fact interested in promoting the common good. A majority of charitable organizations, however, were not launched for the altruistic objective of channelling the company's profits towards general welfare. Often more important was the convenient "side effect" that company profits received by a charitable foundation are exempt from most taxes and are not subject to inheritance tax when the next generation takes control of the company.

The setting up of such charitable foundations follows a simple calculus. In large corporations, annual returns on only 5 or 10 percent of shares will be in the tens or hundreds of millions. That's enough to guarantee a family dynasty, unless overly extended, a life of luxury for a lifetime. Most charitable foundations owning companies are set up so they do not receive any voting rights in the company, or they are controlled by the family itself. Transferring a major part of the company to a charitable foundation by way of such a construction kills three birds with one stone. It ensures that part of the company's profits will not be subject to taxation; it further ensures that the family retains full control of the company and can impose its will; and third, it guarantees a virtually tax-free transfer of the company to its heirs. If, moreover, the foundation facilitates business that helps the company make money, the virtuous circle is closed.

The Bertelsmann Foundation, for instance, has perfected the art of using foundation funds in ways that pay off for the company. Thus the Foundation developed models for the privatization of municipal affairs, implementation of which would then fill the order books of company affiliate Arvato. But even if the funds were spent "only" on the financing of campaigns, think tanks, and other services for influencing public opinion, it would have served its purpose. The fact that today the interests of the richest 1 percent determine political agendas in most countries is of course also a result of who in these countries is capable of financing campaigns and who is not.

Heirs at the receiving end

Many owners transfer their shares to a foundation without worrying about charitable organization status. There will still be tax benefits, such as in the case of inheritance. In such cases, however, tax savings are usually not the main goal. The purpose is to prevent the company from subsequently being stripped, broken up or sold by its heirs, without depriving those same heirs of the benefits of economic feudalism. That's why the statutes of such foundations specify that company profits have to flow to the generation of heirs. The Siepmann Foundation, owned by the retail corporation Aldi Süd, spells out the following in the Bavarian register of foundations: "the purpose of the foundation is that the assets of the foundation and its returns are to be administered according to the will of the founder in order to undertake ongoing or one-time payments ... to the recipients ..." The *recipients* are the heirs of Aldi founder Karl Albrecht.

For this reason, growth in the number of foundations of course does not mean the end of capitalist management philosophy according to which the goal of companies is to pursue maximum profits, and it certainly does not mean an end to capital incomes without work. For the most part, the purpose of foundations is precisely the opposite: protecting the incomes and control of the company for future generations in a tax-optimal fashion.

Abbe establishes the Zeiss Foundation

As mentioned earlier, there is a small number of foundations that are set up in a different way, since their founders were pursuing different goals. One of them is Germany's oldest corporate-supported foundation, the Carl Zeiss Foundation. In 1866, the physicist Ernst Abbe, who was responsible for the foundation's establishment and founding statutes, joined the precision optics works of Carl Zeiss in Jena. Abbe's technological achievement was the construction of a new generation of microscopes of hitherto unknown precision, which meant rapid growth for the company. In 1876 Carl Zeiss promoted his most talented engineer to part owner of the firm. When the founder died twelve years later, Ernst Abbe and the Zeiss heirs became wealthy people.

In the following year, Abbe established the Carl Zeiss Foundation, to which he transferred his own shares and those of the other shareholders that he bought at a premium. With the Zeiss Foundation as the corporate supporter, which in its statute determined management priorities as well as many details concerning work-er-employer relations, Abbe created one of the most successful and at the same time socially responsible companies of his time.

9.3 Profits as a "public good"

Abbe's ideas are surprisingly relevant for our discussion of the basic elements for a model of the modern corporation. In light of the wave of share companies being set up at the time, Abbe was also thinking about what he called the "de-personalization" resulting from the rapid growth of enterprises and what legal model might be appropriate for this situation. He considered both cooperatives and share companies as fitting the bill. "One [i.e. the cooperative] would place the future under the rule of momentary, ephemeral, and to some extent disparate interests of the individuals who happen to be co-members, while the other [i.e. the share company] would end up under the dictate of accumulating money."[101] He considered both ideas wrong.

Abbe saw that the success of a company consists in joining together of the work of many people, both past and present employees, the management skills of upper management, and the technical knowledge and know-how of skilled workers, the results of university research, as well as many decades of society's accumulated knowledge and experience. He was therefore convinced that company profits "ought be viewed and approached from a conception of property as a "public good" based on strict moral standards. The monetary claim of the founder and enterprise director should be limited to "a fair wage for his personal activity."[102]

In Abbe's view, the entire workforce is entitled to a share of company profits. In addition, the company should support those disciplines in the natural sciences from which the optical industry benefited. This is why Abbe decided to transfer the enterprise to a foundation, and in this way make "this third economic factor, i.e. the organization as such"[103], the owner of the enterprise.

With the establishment of the Carl Zeiss Foundation, the founder's heirs lost any influence on the company and any claims for an income without work from company profits. At the same time, the foundation assumed the economic risks, putting an autonomous organization rather than the state in charge of managing the enterprise. However, the statute specified as well that not only Jena University, but also many social institutions in the city would benefit. Thus the Carl Zeiss Foundation financed new university buildings, an evolutionary natural history museum, an anatomical institute, several clinics, and a community centre with a large library.

Ingenious statute for foundations

The charter of the Carl Zeiss Foundation formulated by Ernst Abbe contains a number of ingenious articles of interest to us that certainly contributed to the enterprise's success. Article 40, for example, specified that the goal of the enterprise was not the maximization of profit but rather "an increase in the overall economic return the enterprise is able to guarantee all its members, including the foundation as the owner, with the prospect of its existence in the long run."[104] The foundation statute directed the enterprise to accumulating reserves, internal financing of investments, and strictly limited external debt. In comparison to total profits, the expenditures on common-good objectives were quite limited and significantly lower than returns paid by normal share companies to its shareholders. This model proved its value in economic crisis situations, in particular during the world economic crisis, which on account of its reserves the Carl Zeiss company was able to survive relatively unscathed and with a barely reduced workforce.

The charter prohibited the patenting of inventions made within the enterprise if they had significant value for education and research. The foundation's participation in companies outside the precision optics industry was ruled out. Also of interest is the fact that the charter limited the salaries of management personnel to no more than ten times the average wage. Management was thus only able to achieve higher salaries if it succeeded in raising the wage rates of all employees in the enterprise. In addition, there were a number of regulations for limiting working hours, and establishing holiday and pension benefits, which for the time were revolutionary.

A successful enterprise

Abbe did not think of himself as being on the Left—in fact, he wasn't even a supporter of Social Democracy. His goal was simply to launch a successful enterprise in which profits would be distributed fairly and based on performance rather than following the feudal model. Already in his lifetime, the model worked very well. While in 1875, Carl Zeiss had just 60 employees, at the time of Abbe's death in 1905 the number was more than 1,400. In subsequent decades the enterprise kept growing consistently until it had to be broken up as a result of the Cold War. But neither the absence of external owners nor the relatively narrow spread of income differences were obstacles to success—on the contrary.

Volkswagen started its reconstruction after World War II as an ownerless enterprise under public supervision with strong employee co-determination. Only in 1960 was the auto manufacturer transformed into a private share company, except for the minority veto rights held by the state of Lower Saxony. There is no reason to assume that Volkswagen would be building lower-quality cars if this transformation had not occurred.

We have examined the growing role of foundations in the economy today, and specifically the legacy of Ernst Abbe, in such detail because both demonstrate that there is a host of other possibilities for structuring economic property and the charter of enterprises in addition to the unfruitful choice between private economy and state economy. The key to a more innovative, productive and at the same time more just economy does not lie in the transformation of commercial enterprises into state-owned ones, just as the private owner entrepreneur is not the main actor in our capitalist economy today.

Neutralization of capital

After World War II, a number of West German economists, such as Alfred Weber, discussed whether the Carl Zeiss Foundation might not serve as a general model for a modern, democratic arrangement of economic ownership. This debate, later picked up by Czech reformer Ota Šik and even parts of the German Free Democratic (liberal) Party, occurred in part under the heading of *"capital neutralization"*. For Ota Šik, the neutralization of capital meant "transferring monetary and productive capital into an indivisible asset"[105] belonging to the enterprise as a whole, that cannot be bought, sold, bequeathed, or arbitrarily destroyed by anyone. This capital would thus no longer be an object of ownership in the traditional sense—rather, ownership rights would be *neutralized.*

The argument is based on the basic observation already formulated by Ernst Abbe, that an enterprise is fundamentally different from a car or a residential home. Enterprises are not *things*, but *organizations* that grow on account of the labour and the knowledge of many people, and the continued existence of which determines the fate of these people as well as of entire regions. For normal items of use, in addition to being an individual right, it makes sense to leave it up to the owner's whim whether to sell, bequeath, give away, or destroy them. With respect to larger enterprises, such individual rights are difficult to defend. The situation becomes completely absurd when such ownership rights are claimed for enterprises that benefit from public funds in one way or another.

Enterprises, along with their assets, grow mainly as a result of re-investing profits and on account of additional purchasing power from loans. External infusions of capital may occur at times of rapid growth or in crisis situations. However, as a rule, in larger enterprises only a minimal share of total capital derives from external capital investments. The rest emerges within the enterprise from the work performed—and in part thanks to diverse state subsidies.

The demand for "capital neutralization" refers to this newly formed capital, which according to current law is automatically transferred to the external capital investor. "Capital neutralization" would mean that instead this newly formed capital becomes the distinct property of the enterprise, while external capital investors as well as external creditors will receive an interest yield on their capital, which in case of higher risk would be correspondingly higher. Such an arrangement would be the logical counterpart to limited liability.

9.4 Entrepreneurial freedom without neo-feudalism

We will return to these proposals in our model of a modern economic order. But first let us restate the basic question: What should a productive, innovative, and at the same time just economic order be able to provide? The answer can be summed up in one sentence: It should guarantee the freedom of entrepreneurial initiative while at the same time avoiding the neo-feudal consequences of today's economic ownership—incomes without work and the possibility to inherit control over an enterprise. In concrete terms, this means that talented founders with workable ideas will get a chance irrespective of their origin—that is, access to capital would be democratized. Once capital is no longer a monopoly asset of a small segment of society, capital incomes will also disappear. In addition, a modern economic order needs barriers to prevent economic property rights from turning into instruments of power, circumventing democracy and imposing the interests of a privileged group on society as a whole.

Based on these criteria, I will suggest four legal forms of enterprise that are designed to replace the share company: personal liability company, employee-owned enterprise, public corporation, and common-good enterprise. They differ from each other, since different sectors of the economy present different requirements for firm size and public participation.

Personal liability company: getting rich with full risk

Personal liability companies are already in existence. These are enterprises in which the owner usually starts out with her own money and is fully liable for any obligations incurred by the enterprise. For starting a cafe, an artisanal firm, or a domestic services company, as a rule no external venture capital or public subsidies are needed. Often personal savings plus bank loans are enough, especially if several people join together. For the owners, choosing this approach to starting an enterprise means taking on the full risk. If the start-up fails, they will often lose everything they have. Taking on this kind of risk and in the end succeeding give you the opportunity to get rich. A free entrepreneur, however, will not receive any public funds, credit guarantees, grants, or other subsidies as long as the enterprise remains the private property of a personal liability company.

If at some point the owner would like to take advantage of public funding, it will be necessary to transform the enterprise into a employee-owned company. In a healthy enterprise, this step can be taken at any time for other reasons as well, for instance that the founder is no longer willing to carry the risk of personal liability in a growing enterprise, or because there is a need for more capital as a result of the firm's rapid expansion. Of course, another motive is also conceivable, one that plays a role today in the establishment of foundations—to keep heirs from breaking up the business, or not to burden its substance with a high inheritance tax. In the move from a personal liability company to an employee-owned company, the original owner is paid back the initially invested capital (but not its growth in the business) with interest, paid out gradually over time.

Employee-owned company: can't be sold or milked

An employee-owned company is not an enterprise in which employees own private shares. An employee-owned company does not have any external owners—like a foundation, nobody owns it. An enterprise in the legal form of an employee-owned company thus belongs to itself, and in this sense it is owned by its workforce as a whole. However, it is not individual property in the current understanding of ownership rights that can be sold or bequeathed.

In an enterprise without any external owners, only three things will change immediately. First, there is nobody who could sell the enterprise or parts of it, and therefore nobody is able to buy it. It thus ceases to be a commodity and a takeover target that financial investors or competitors could get their hands on and cannibalize. Second, there will be nobody who can claim profits as a result of ownership. This eliminates the pressure to pay out dividends, which can be put to better use for investments into a long-term growth strategy. A third difference is that in an enterprise without external owners, a new solution has to be found for who will direct the enterprise, decide on its goals, and control it. Because this is precisely what those who own the business, or their representatives on the board of directors, do today.

Control as the sole ownership right

In order to guard against negligent or simply underperforming executives and managers, there is no need for external owners, as successful companies fully owned by foundations demonstrate. What is needed are controlling organs staffed by people whose fate is closely connected with that of the company, and whose interests are in line with a positive, stable, and successful development of the enterprise.

For today's owners of enterprises, this is often not the case. Financial funds, private equity and other institutional investors who keep moving from one company to the next, are above all interested in short-term profits. In the ideal case, family heirs are interested in the company's long-term success, but they frequently exert pressure for increased dividend payments, want to be bought out, which negatively affects the firm's substance, or create uncertainty as a result of drawn-out family feuds.

If instead the different parts of the workforce—from unskilled workers to skilled workers and higher-level employees—send elected representatives to the controlling organ, this will ensure that the interests of the workforce as a whole will be taken into account. Smaller enterprises up to 50 employees can do without elected representatives. There the employees simply *are* the general assembly, which decides who will lead the enterprise and sets company goals.

Larger companies of course need what they already have today: clear lines of authority and hierarchies based on qualification. The operative management, like any other professional activity, should be in the hands of individuals with the necessary skills and knowledge. But this is not directly related to the question of the firm's ownership. Obviously, employees are not able to manage their enterprises by way of majority decisions in daily general assemblies.

Of the classical ownership rights, an employee-owned enterprise will retain only one—the right to control the enterprise and its management. Whereas today this authority is in the hand of external owners, in an employee-owned enterprise it is exercised by the workforce.

Interested in long-term success

Since all employees will earn more if the business is doing well, and less if sales take a plunge, and since all have an interest in job security in the long run, directions to management would look something like this: strong sales, solid profits, though not at the price of pitiful wages and precarious jobs, a high rate of investment, and long-term growth of the enterprise rather than short-term pursuit of high profits.

A manager who is able to double the company's net worth while reducing the workforce by half in all likelihood will not be celebrated as a hero in the general assembly. The CEO, on the other hand, who compensates for the use of labour-saving technologies by reducing working hours or through employee retraining and new growth strategies will stand a good chance of having his contract renewed.

This does not mean that an employee-owned company that is in the red for an extended period of time may not have to eliminate jobs. However, under such conditions cutting jobs would be the last measure rather than, as is the case today, the first and preferred means of saving the enterprise. And where today job cuts have driving up capital returns as their only purpose, they would be ruled out in the future. The same applies to replacing well-paid, regular jobs with temporary and contract workers, or relocating in order to save wage costs.

Motivated employees

There are strong arguments that this form of enterprise would motivate employees much more strongly to do good work than is the case in the current system. "When a firm is transformed into a community as a result of greater participation, productivity increases as well," Richard Wilkinson, a scholar of inequality, has found in numerous studies. In an employee-owned company, employees would not only participate in decision-making, but would work exclusively for themselves instead of underwriting the company heir's Porsche.

Individual cases demonstrate that employee-owned companies can function even under legal conditions that are quite unfavourable to this model. For the most part, these are cases with particularly poor starting conditions. Company takeovers by employees occurred in most cases after former owners drove the enterprise into bankruptcy, with employees attempting to save what they could. In the 1980s, for instance, there were 40 cases of such employee takeovers in Germany, 15 of which were successful in securing jobs in the long term.

On the whole, there are 7,000 enterprises in Germany with complete or majority employee ownership, among them 1,800 *cooperatives*. A problem of current legal ownership forms is that as a rule ownership is not tied to active participation in the enterprise, but rather represents personal ownership. Thus it is possible to take away shares when leaving the enterprise and also for others to inherit them. The same is true when employees receive shares in a limited liability company or employee shares. In addition, in all of these ownership forms it is possible to pay out part of the profits, and as a result there is pressure to do just that. It is not really what our model is about. What such examples demonstrate conclusively is that successful management is also possible in enterprises owned by its employees, even under generally adverse legal and economic conditions.

Public risk fund

Those who on their own or along with others take the initiative to set up an employee-owned company would have an opportunity to receive the necessary starting capital from a public risk fund. Such a fund should be made available at the level of 1 percent of GNP, to be financed from a profit tax levied on all businesses. Alternatively, an employee-owned company could be set up using—in addition or exclusively—private funds which would be paid back with interest once the enterprise is up and running. This would be an obligation to be fulfilled independently of the shareholder assembly's decisions, comparable to the right of banks to receive back their loans with interest.

The larger an enterprise becomes, the stronger its effects on the interests of society as a whole, not just on its own employees. In addition to employee representatives, enterprises of a certain size should include municipal representatives, and further down the road individuals appointed by other levels of government, to participate and vote in employee assemblies. Especially if enterprises benefit significantly from public funding, this should go hand in hand with greater influence of public interests.

The Public Company: public participation

For large enterprises operating in oligopolistic markets that are almost by definition economically powerful, the employee-owned company is not an appropriate model. For enterprises of this kind I suggest the legal form of Public Company. Like employee-owned enterprises, public companies do not have external owners. Here too, the company owns itself rather than being owned by the state. What distinguishes a public company from an employee-owned enterprise is the composition of the controlling body. It would have a board of directors, only half of whom will be employee representatives. The other half will consist of representatives of the general public, appointed by municipalities and regions in which the company conducts its operations.

Of course, determining such limits of size that specify at what size a company becomes a public concern is always fraught with difficulty and to some extent arbitrary. However, no one can deny that there is a difference between a window manufacturer and the Volkswagen Corporation, or between a cafe in one city and the global Starbucks chain. An enterprise with 2,000 employees is a major actor in its community. In order to play a key role at the level of a country as a whole, however, the enterprise needs to be significantly larger.

Employee-owned companies with more than 1,000 employees would be required to include a municipal representative in their employee assembly, while larger companies or those with public funding would have a proportionately greater number of municipal representatives. Enterprises with more than 20,000 employees could not take the legal form of employee-owned company or personal liability company (few of the latter type currently exist). This would be the domain of public companies. Public companies will also be commercial enterprises under professional management and with a profit orientation. In contrast to employee-owned companies, their goals and investment priorities cannot be established without the endorsement of public representatives and thus the public at large. This is a way of taking into account the public weight of such enterprises, which on account of public share ownership would also have public representatives on their boards of directors.

At present, there are a number of enterprises that as a result of public share ownership have representatives of the public on their boards. The most famous example is the Volkswagen Corporation, in which the state of Lower Saxony has minority veto power. It would be difficult to make the case that this public influence has ever constituted an obstacle to successful management. At the same time, it is obviously no guarantee for proper management, as the current emissions scandal shows.

Common-good company: social services

The fourth legal form of enterprise proposed here is the common-good company. It would be appropriate for any sector that is not suitable for commercial management—such as those tied to networks or where network effects occur (or both)—and that have a tendency towards monopolization, or where goods and services concern basic human needs that should be equally accessible to all rather than being based on purchasing power.

Common-good companies are established with public funds and, much like non-state social agencies as well as some municipal enterprises today, are not profit-oriented. They should fulfil their mandate on a cost recovery basis. Common-good companies are also not owned by the state, but are in self-ownership. They operate according to specific rules and under public control, but no one is allowed to arbitrarily interfere in their work. Since the state does not own them, the state cannot sell them, i. e. they cannot be privatized.

We have witnessed for many years how a range of negative effects emerge when handing over a municipality's water supply or hospitals to commercial enterprises interested primarily in turning a profit. Where markets do not work and where there can be no serious competition, different rules have to be applied. As discussed in the chapter on common-good banks, on account of its key economic position, the banking sector should be dominated by institutions under the legal form of common-good companies.

High-speed Internet for all

The same should apply to communication services and particularly the infrastructure of the digital economy. In Germany and other countries the expansion of high-speed networks has slowed because thinly populated regions are not attractive for profit-oriented suppliers. Wireless connections too are weak or overloaded in many locations. In fact, this sector is a perfect example for the theory of economist Harold Hotelling. The cheapest alternative for supplying Internet, telephony, and television is the public construction of networks in the hands of a non-profit common-good company. Under such conditions, Internet access would not have to be restricted but could be available to anyone anytime. Each household would pay a monthly fee that would be considerably lower than the communications expenses of an average household today, while nevertheless guaranteeing cost-effective maintenance and ongoing updating of the network structure.

The digital world also needs common-good oriented suppliers. We saw earlier that there are two ways to make money with digital information: either artificial reduction of the supply and sale of information (so far not a very successful variant), or storing the personal data of customers and users,which can then be profitably exploited. If something that can be multiplied at no cost is kept artificially scarce, this is not a particularly good solution—even if in certain areas, such as for maintaining quality journalism on the Internet, there may be no other way. If, on the other hand, our life is stored more and more comprehensively and exhaustively on the servers of data monopolists, we will lose even more—our freedom and our privacy.

No escaping ...

"There will be no escaping once surveillance systems have taken over our residences, cars, and electronic appliances,"[106] writes IT expert Yvonne Hofstetter. This kind of excessive surveillance can be prevented only through strict regulations ensuring automatic and prompt deletion of all data. It is high time for laws on what and for how long the servers of the data monsters are permitted to store our data. One idea would be a commitment to delete our digital tracks automatically and completely within a few days—with the exception of what we ourselves have explicitly decided to store. However, this would eliminate the basis of the commercial business model in many areas of the digital economy. This model would therefore have to be replaced by publicly financed, non-profit oriented providers. Otherwise we might be required to pay for every click on a search engine or for opening an account on a social network, which would be the commercial alternative to the use of our data.

This is also about avoiding dependency and the concentration of power. The digital networks are the most important infrastructure for future industry. With every further step in the digitalization of the value-added chain, the question who controls these networks will become more pressing. If control is left to private monopolists, their power position may be exploited in a way that is lethal for any market economy. There is in fact no rational alternative to strictly regulated common-good providers. Why, for example, should internet trading not occur on a public portal that simply provides a smart software for connecting buyers and sellers without making a large profit and exploiting our data? The more digitalization is advancing in our cars, homes, and life in general, the more urgent is a common-good oriented new beginning in dealing with digital technology.

Reduced to the smallest size

The economic order proposed here would be characterized by four basic types of enterprises, depending on the composition of the market and the public relevance of individual sectors: Personal-liability companies, employee-owned companies, public enterprises, and common-good enterprises. Transforming current corporations into these new legal forms would be relatively simple. The externally provided capital in a company will be calculated with interest. Payments received in the past will be subtracted. If this calculation shows that an investor has put more money into the company than she has withdrawn, the difference will be paid from profits. The internally generated capital belongs to the company. In reality it is unlikely that there will be many cases where future payments will be due since normally—especially in the case of older companies—past payments have far exceeded the capital invested.

All enterprises with the exception of common-good companies will be commercial, profit-oriented businesses. A modern economic order therefore needs a market constitution that reduces enterprises to their smallest technologically feasible size. Of course, in many economic sectors, only large enterprises will survive. But there is no need for global manufacturing or trading giants with interlinked ownership structures that are profitable for their shareholders primarily because they eliminate competition, dominate suppliers, and reduce choices for customers.

In order to provide incentives for enterprises to adopt innovative, cost-effective, and productive technologies, open markets and intense competition are needed. Market actors that want to stay ahead of their competition should achieve this through technological superiority, high quality, or simply the discovery of a new market niche. At the same time, strict (rather than today's strongly diluted) environmental and consumer protection legislation should ensure that cost-cutting technologies at the expense of the public will not be permitted. This degree of control is something that the market and competition cannot produce.

Deconcentration

The transformation of corporations into employee-owned enterprises or public companies should be linked directly to a process of deconcentration. This would finally fulfil the demand that Walter Eucken, head of the liberal Freiburg School of Economics, had formulated already at the end of World War II: "Conglomerates, trusts, and monopolistic enterprises should be broken up or dissolved unless there are technological or economic conditions that would make this impossible."[107] The first draft of a new cartel law, the Josten proposal drawn up under Ludwig Erhard between 1946 and 1949, explicitly called for measures of deconcentration. "Individual companies with economic power" were to be broken up into self-sustaining enterprises. As was to be expected, economic lobbyists strongly opposed this idea—successfully so. In a government proposal published in 1952, deconcentration measures had already disappeared. Ludwig Erhard had buckled under the opposition of powerful economic actors, much to the dismay of his former liberal friends and their supporters. But the problem remains relevant, even more so today than in the 1950s. The largest enterprises of that time were small compared to the global giants of today.

Reducing the size of companies and eliminating overlapping and interlinked ownership structures would also make it easier to collect taxes from companies. Taxes on profits should be high enough to contribute to the financing of common-good companies. Individuals caring for others in hospitals and care facilities, for example, would as a result no longer earn less than engineers.

Such enterprises reduced in size should easily be able to survive competition with the remaining global giants with which they would be forced to compete until other countries have instituted similar changes. Precisely because they will not be pressured by shareholders siphoning off capital, expecting minimum returns of 16 percent, they will be able to make better and more durable products based on larger investments in quality and innovation. The Saarstahl steel company, which is relatively small in its sector, is in the hands of a foundation. Precisely for this reason it has more investment funds available and so far has been able to survive competition with large steel corporations without serious problems. The monetary order proposed here would represent another competitive advantage as a result of improved funding opportunities.

Property only through individual work

The model of a modern economic order proposed here would pave the way for an economy in which property can in fact only come into being as a result of personal work and in which feudal structures and incomes without work will be a thing of the past. Our economic life would become more innovative, more flexible, and at the same time more socially just. No one would be in a position to become rich from the work of others and at the expense of others. Genuine markets and free competition would be much more relevant than they are today—but of course only where they can work and are ethically defensible. We could run our polity democratically again, without the uncontrollable meddling of corporate giants.

Capitalism is not without an alternative. On the contrary, if we want to live in a free, democratic, innovative, prosperous, and just society, we have to overcome capitalist economic feudalism. Based on a new economic ownership system, which limits greed and simply makes unrestrained self-enrichment at the expense of others impossible, we will ultimately all be more prosperous.

Only on the basis of a new economic order will we succeed in making digital technologies useful for a better life for us all and in getting closer to the goal of producing our wealth in harmony with our natural environment.

ACKNOWLEDGEMENTS

Special thanks go to Lorenz Jarass, who advises, among others, the European Commission, the European Parliament and the German Federal Parliament, for project coordination and document creation. He has published 14 books and more than 100 articles and has supported this edition with his expertise.

And thank you to Gustav M. Obermair for his commitment. He is a former president of the University of Regensburg, Germany, and has published several books and more than 50 articles in leading international journals.

ENDNOTES

1 Oxfam, An Economy for the 1 percent. January 2016.

2 Franklin D. Roosevelt, Speech in Madison Square Garden, 31 October 1936.

3 Friedrich A. Hayek, Individualism and Economic Order, University of Chicago Press 1996, pp. 267–269.

4 Ibid., p. 260.

5 J.M. Keynes, "National Self-Sufficiency", Yale Review Vol. 22, No. 4 (June 1933), 755–769.

6 Byung-Chul Han, Duft der Zeit: Ein philosophischer Essay zur Kunst des Verweilens, Bielefeld 2015.

7 Richard Wilkinson and Kate Pickett, The Spirit Level: Why Greater Equality Makes Societies Stronger, Bloomsbury Publishers 2011.

8 Ibid.

9 Karl Polanyi, The Great Transformation. The Political and Economic Origins of Our Time. Beacon Press 2001, p. 48.

10 Chrystia Freeland, Plutocrats: The Rise of the New Global Super-Rich and the Fall of Everyone Else, Penguin Press 2012, p. 410.

11 Quoted in Sven Beckert, Empire of Cotton. A Global History. New York: Knopf 2014.

12 Jared Lanier, Who Owns the Future? Simon and Schuster 2013.

13 Peter Thiel, Zero to One. Notes on Startups and How to Build the Future. Crown Business 2014, p. 17.

14 John Maynard Keynes, Essays in Persuasion, New York: W. W. Norton & Co., 1963, pp. 367, 369.

15 www.gruene-bundestag.de/uploads/tx_ttproducts/dat018_obsoleszenz.pdf

16 www.gegenblende.de/++co++1e747c5e-11e3-96bf-52540066f352

17 Christian Felber, Geld. Die neuen Spielregeln. Wien 2014, p. 161.

18 Handelsblatt, 17 June 2015.

19 Quoted in Mariana Mazzucato, Das Kapital des Staates, p. 228.

20 www.patentverein.de/files/Frauenhofer_102003.pdf

21 Hermann Simon, Hidden Champions des 21. Jahrhunderts. Frankfurt am Main 2007.

22 www.gegenblende.de/++co++1e747c5e-11e3-96bf-52540066f352

23   Thomas Piketty, Capital in the Twenty-first Century. The Belknap Press 2014, p. 443.

24   Ibid, p. 814.

25   Ibid, p. 501.

26   Chrystia Freeland, Plutocrats: The Rise of the New Global Super-Rich and the Fall of Everyone Else, Penguin Press 2012, p. 145.

27   Thomas Piketty, Capital in the Twenty-first Century. The Belknap Press 2014.

28   Quoted in Jürgen Kocka, Geschichte des Kapitalismus. Munich 2013.

29   Joseph A. Schumpeter, Capitalism, Socialism, and Democracy. Harper, 3rd ed. 2008, p. 16.

30   Michael Hartmann, Eliten und Macht in Europa. Frankfurt am Main 2007, p. 149.

31   Ibid., p. 144.

32   Ibid., p. 146.

33   Thomas Piketty, Capital in the Twenty-First Century. Cambridge, MA 2014, p. 246.

34   Handelsblatt, 17 March 2014.

35   Alex Capus, Patriarchen. Zehn Portraits. 5th ed. Klagenfurt 2008, p. 12.

36   Thierry Volery, Ev Müllner, Visionäre, die sich durchsetzen. Zürich 2006.

37   Bernt Engelmann, Das Reich zerfiel, die Reichen blieben. Munich 1975., p. 59.

38   John Stuart Mill, Principles of Political Economy with some of their Applications to Social Philosophy (1848), Book II, Ch. II, http://www.econlib.org/library/Mill/mlP15.html#Bk.II,Ch.II

39   Alexander Rüstow, Die Religion der Marktwirtschaft, Vol. 4, 3rd ed., Berlin 2009, p. 96.

40   Johann Wolfgang Goethe, West-East Divan: Poems, with "Notes and Essays" (1819), Albany, NY 2010, p. 217.

41   Adam Smith, The Wealth of Nations (1776), London and New York 1991, pp. 406, 117.

42   Fernand Braudel, Afterthoughts on Material Civilization and Capitalism. The Johns Hopkins University Press, 1977.

43   Die Zeit, 1 May 1959.

44   Handelsblatt, 4 November 2014.

45   Barry C. Lynn, Cornered. The New Monopoly Capitalism and the Economics of Destruction, Hoboken 2010, pl XII.

46   Stefania Vitali, James B. Glattfelder and Stefano Battiston, "The network of global corporate control", Zurich 2011. http://arxiv.org/pdf/1107.5728.pdf

47   Ulrike Herrmann, Der Sieg des Kapitals. Frankfurt am Main 2013, p. 68.

48   Carl Shapiro and Hal R. Varian, Information Rules: A Strategic Guide to the Network Economy. Boston: Harvard Business School Press, 1994, p. 15.

49   Ibid., p. 59.

50   Ibid., p. 64

51   Walter Eucken, Grundsätze der Wirtschaftspolitik. Tübingen 2004, p. 172.

52   Quoted in Jeremy Rifkin, The Zero Marginal Cost Society. St. Martin's Press 2014.

53   Cf. Christoph Keese, Silicon Valley. Munich 2014.

54   Yvonne Hofstetter, Sie wissen alles. Munich 2014, p. 219.

55   Milton Friedman, Capitalism and Freedom. University of Chicago Press, 1968.

56   Fernand Braudel, Afterthoughts on Material Civilization and Capitalism. The Johns Hopkins University Press, 1977, p. 64.

57   Ibid., p. 57.

58   Goethe, Faust: parts 1 and 2, translated by Albert G. Latham, London 1912, p. 307.

59   Sven Beckert, Empire of Cotton. A Global History. New York: Knopf, 2014.

60   Karl Polanyi. The Great Transformation. The Political and Economic Origins of Our Time. Beacon Press 2001, p. 217.

61   Ibid., p. 258.

62   Mariana Mazzucato, Das Kapital des Staates. Munich 2014, p. 22.

63   Handelsblatt, 23 September 2014.

64   Wirtschaftswoche No. 1/2, 9 January 2012.

65   Spiegel Online, 29 October 2014.

66   Peter Thiel, Zero to One. Notes on Startups and How to Build the Future. Crown Business 2014, p. 38.

67   Ibid., p. 149.

68   Joseph Schumpeter, The Theory of Economic Development. Transaction Publishers 1983.

69   Quoted in Hans D. Barbier and Fides Krause-Brewer (eds.), Die Person hinter dem Produkt. 40 Porträts erfolgreicher Unternehmer. Bonn 1987, p. 274.

70   Ibid., p. 227.

71   Jeremy Rifkin, The Zero Marginal Cost Society. St. Martin's Press 2014, pp. 660–661.

72   Alexander Rüstow et al., Das Versagen des Wirtschaftsliberalismus. Marburg 2001, p. 121.

73   Ibid., p. 94.

74   Ludwig Erhard and Franz Oppenheimer. "Dem Lehrer und Freund" in Karl Hohmann and Ludwig Erhard, Gedanken aus fünf Jahrzehnten, Reden und Schriften. Düsseldorf 1990, pp. 858–864.

75   Translator: W. K. Marriott. Release Date: February 11, 2006 [EBook #1232]. http://www.gutenberg.org/files/1232/1232-h/1232-h.htm. Last updated: July 11, 2016.

76   Fernand Braudel, Afterthoughts on Material Civilization and Capitalism. The Johns Hopkins University Press, 1977, p. 72.

77   Steven Johnson, Where good ideas come from. A natural history of innovation. Riverhead Books 2010.

78   Ibid.

79   Ibid.

80   Carl Benedikt Frey and Michael A. Osborne, The Future of Employment: How Susceptible are Jobs to Computerisation? 17 September 2013. www.oxfordmartin.ox.ac.uk

81   Quoted in Robert and Edward Skidelsky, Wie viel ist genug? Munich 2013, p. 289.

82   Anat Admati and Martin Hellwig, Des Bankers neue Kleider. Munich 2013, p. 38.

83   Quoted in Christian Felber, Geld. Die neuen Spielregeln. Vienna 2014, p. 22.

84   Joseph Stiglitz, The Price of Inequality. How Today's Divided Society Endangers Our Future. W.W. Norton, p. 142.

85   See inter alia Daniel Stelter, Die Schulden im 21. Jahrhundert. Frankfurt am Main, 2014, p. 78.

86   Karl Polanyi, The Great Transformation.The Political and Economic Origins of Our Time. Beacon Press 2001, p. 237.

87   Ibid., p. 238.

88   For empirical evidence, see the study by Richard A. Werner: http://inflationsschutzbrief.de/studien/richard-werner-studie-koennen-einzelne-banken-geld-aus-dem-nichts-schoepfen

89   On the methods, see Dirk Sollte, Weltfinanzsystem am Limit. Einblicke in den 'Heiligen Gral' der Globalisierung. Berlin 2009.

90   Walter Eucken, Grundsätze der Wirtschaftspolitik. Tübingen 2004, p. 4.

91   World Bank, The East Asian Miracle. Economic Growth and Public Policy. 1993.   http://documents.worldbank.org/curated/en/975081468244550798/Main-report

92   Study of the "Tax Justice Network" at http://www.taxjustice.net/cms/upload/pdf/Price_of_Offshore_Revisited_120722.pdf

93   See Jean-Jacques Rousseau, Discourse on the Origin of Inequality. Hackett Publishing 1992.

94   Pierre-Joseph Proudhon, What is Property? Edited by Donald R. Kelley and Bonnie J. Smith. Cambridge University Press, 1994.

95   See Martin Nettesheim and Stefan Thomas, Entflechtung im deutschen Kartellrecht. Tübingen 2011.

96   Adam Smith, An Inquiry into the Nature and Causes of the Wealth of Nations. Bantam Classics, 2003, Book III, Ch. 2, p. 851.

97   Quoted in Werner Plumpe (ed.), Eine Vision, zwei Unternehmen. 125 Jahre Carl-Zeiss-Stiftung. Munich 2014, p. 14. Handelsblatt, 24 November 2014.

98   Die Welt, 18 February 2011.

99   Handelsblatt, 24 November 2014.

100   Joseph A. Schumpeter, Capitalism, Socialism, and Democracy. Harper, 3rd ed. 2008.

101   Werner Plumpe (ed.), Eine Vision, zwei Unternehmen. 125 Jahre Carl-Zeiss-Stiftung. Munich 2014, p. 15.

102   Ibid., pp. 45–46.

103   Ibid., p. 45.

104   Ibid., p. 114.

105   Ota Šik, Humane Wirtschaftsdemokratie. Ein Dritter Weg. Hamburg 1979, p. 15.

106   Yvonne Hofstetter, Sie wissen alles. Munich 2014, p. 224.

107   Walter Eucken, Wirtschaftsmacht und Wirtschaftsordnung. Berlin 2012, p. 86.